In praise of *Crave*...

"Tired of fluffy books on the spiritual life? Chris Tomlinson has written a biblical, God-centered antidote. *Crave* takes us on a frank and honest journey through the challenges of the Christian walk in today's world. It is at once a wise, practical, and readable guide, useful for those who recognize spiritual mediocrity in themselves but want to grow beyond it."

Duane Litfin
president, Wheaton College

"In this creative blend of autobiography and devotional, Chris Tomlinson paints for us a Christ who satisfies our cravings for Himself. An inspiring work from a gifted and anointed writer."

Christian George
author of *Sacred Travels*; *Sex, Sushi, & Salvation*; and *Godology*

"Chris Tomlinson addresses the noblest and most necessary question in the most disarming style. It is the theme that engaged the best thoughts of writers from Augustine to Pascal to C.S. Lewis. It explores what Pascal called the 'God-shaped vacuum': How do we satisfy our hunger for God? No mortal can answer the question with finality. But this book takes us a long way in the right direction."

Ronnie Collier Stevens
Danube International Church
Budapest, Hungary

"Chris Tomlinson possesses a skill rare in Christian writing today: a clean, clear, powerf~~ ~~ sneaky comedic sens~~ ~~ never say it himself, ~~ ~~ to learn."

editor i~~ ~~

"An honest exploration of doubts, fears, missteps and victories from an authentic, not-yet-arrived follower of Christ."

Rev. Joseph Pensak
campus minister, Reformed University Fellowship

*

"Written with an enjoyable and attractive vulnerability, this book will draw many of us to places we've wanted to go in our relationships with God but have struggled to find because of the clutter of life. I love the way *Crave* challenges cultural and comfortable Christianity, both in how we internally experience the reality of Christ and externally express the gospel to the world around us."

David Robbins
regional director, Campus Crusade for Christ

*

"*Crave* is part autobiography, part theological musing. Chris talks about God in a very personal and compelling manner. His message is clear and told through the introspective and often hilarious experiences of his own life: that God is great and should be praised. An engrossing read that not only had me laughing out loud but also thinking about my own personal beliefs, even from an atheist's perspective."

Andy Wang
friend and atheist

Crave

chris tomlinson

HARVEST HOUSE PUBLISHERS

EUGENE, OREGON

Cover by Left Coast Design, Portland, Oregon

Cover and interior photos © Shutterstock; iStockphoto

Backcover author photo by K.W. @ www.KatWillcox.com

CRAVE
Copyright © 2010 by Chris Tomlinson
Published by Harvest House Publishers
Eugene, Oregon 97402
www.harvesthousepublishers.com

Library of Congress Cataloging-in-Publication Data

Tomlinson, Chris
Crave / Chris Tomlinson.
   p. cm.
   ISBN 978-0-7369-2693-5 (pbk.)
   1. Spirituality. I. Title.
   BV4501.3.T657 2010
   248.4—dc22

                                                        2009019089

Printed in the United States of America

         10 11 12 13 14 15 16 17 18 / VP-NI / 10 9 8 7 6 5 4 3 2 1

To Jesus Christ—
Lord, may You satisfy every craving of my soul.

Acknowledgments

Writing a book seems like such an individual kind of thing. Before I wrote this one, I always imagined writers sitting alone at their typewriters, pounding out thoughts until their books were complete. And then these books magically went from the typewriters onto bookstore shelves and finally into my hands. Little did I know that it takes a team, and a large one at that, to pull together even a simple book like this one. These acknowledgments are not much of a show of my gratitude, but they will have to suffice.

First, I would like to thank Jesus for the gift of words. I love reading words, and I'm finding I love writing them as well. To be able to write is a gift, and I give all the credit to the Giver.

Next, I would like to thank some of the folks who helped to start this entire process. Thanks to Donald Anderson for being the first person I can remember telling me I could and should write. Many thanks to Jordan Green and Penny Carothers for giving me space to find my voice at the beginning. Thanks also to Pam Guerrieri for some early encouragement in the writing of this book. And to some of my close friends who walked with me at the start of this journey, thank you for your patience and encouragement. These men read mercifully through the first draft of the manuscript, which had a really bad working title and not much better writing, and they provided the right kind of encouragement to put shape and form to something that desperately needed it. Thank you, Andy Black, for your encouragement to write in the first place. Thank you, James Anderson, for bringing your storyteller's eye to these stories. Thank you, Billy Orme, for being a soul-deep brother who sharpens me and my writing whenever we meet. Thank you, Matt Rillos—Mr. Encouragement—for being so excited about this book.

I'd also like to thank Bill Anderson for cracking open the door. Thanks to Bob Hawkins Jr. for running a company that proclaims Jesus as the answer to every human need. I feel deeply indebted to Bob, LaRae Weikert, John Constance, Barb Sherrill, and Terry Glaspey for taking a shot with this book. I hope it merits the honor you've shown to it. To Terry, your gut-level insight into the heart of this book brought it to life. Thanks to Gene Skinner for your careful editing of this manuscript and the job you did polishing these words. And thanks to Betty Fletcher, Shane White, Katie Lane, Christianne Debysingh, Dave Bartlett, Abby Van Wormer, Elizabeth Colclough, Bryce Williamson, Daniel Hawkins, Pat Mathis, and the rest of the wonderful people at Harvest House who formed the backbone of this team.

To the Outlet and the Newmen, thank you for living life with me and helping to create many of these stories. To the Seven—Jami Valentine, Nickki Peavey, Allison Dybdahl, Tim Reeves, Melissa Mollner, Erik Svendsen, and Lacey Baker—thank you for the feedback party, and what a party it was! To my family—Mom, Dad, Scott, Tracy, M2, D2, Cara, Matt, and Aaron—you make life worth writing about. And to Anna, my muse, my delight, and my most trusted editor, you make life worth living.

Finally, to you, the reader, thank you for joining me on this journey. I'm grateful you would spend this time with me, and I hope you've found some sort of encouragement from what you have read. Nothing would make me happier than for you to leave this book wanting to make much of Jesus, and I hope you and I will have the chance to meet, either in the here and now or in the there and then.

Contents

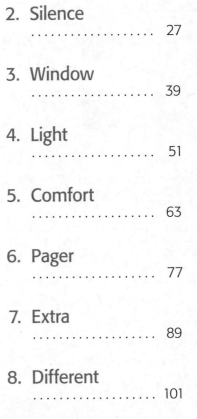

Beginning:

The Cravings Begin

I am staring at a chubby kid eating ice cream, and the experience is deeply profound.

Before you think ill of me, you should know that this boy is actually on my television, or more specifically, on a picture that is taped to my television. With his brow furrowed and his right hand tightly gripping a spoon, he is sitting in front of a large carton of ice cream, the spoon buried deep below its surface. His eyes reveal the intensity of deep desire; in that moment, all that exists in the world is his mouth, a spoon, and the ice cream. As if his expression didn't convey it clearly enough, the creators of this image have named his desire in large white letters spread across the scene: CRAVE.

In this case, a picture is not worth a thousand words, but simply one, and that word is *crave.*

My wife, Anna, put it on our TV because she thinks it's a really cute picture. But she also taped it there as a reminder for us to crave the things of God, particularly when we would rather sit on the couch and watch a movie. I need this constant reminder to crave more of God, mostly because I have spiritual ADHD. My heart is much like that of Methodist pastor Robert Robinson, who wrote, "Let Thy goodness, like a fetter, / Bind my wandering heart to Thee. / Prone to wander, Lord, I feel it, / Prone to leave the God I love."[1] Robinson speaks old words into my young heart, and as I walk the path of life, my heart desires the goodness of God's presence but all too easily wanders away from Him in search of God knows what.

It has been this way for most of my Christian life, which began after a family Bible study when I was eight. The following years were not marked by a craving of the kind evidenced by my chubby young friend but instead were filled with a distinctly Western, Evangelical kind of life, filled to the brim with both orthodoxy and complacency.

I have always loved God and enjoyed learning about the Bible. My teenage years were packed with youth group activities and mission trips and hardly any trouble. But this was the sum total of my Christian faith: reading my Bible, going to church, staying out of trouble, and going on mission trips. It sounds like a good upbringing, and it was, but I didn't have anything that came close to a life filled with an all-consuming desire for God. My faith was just one part of my life, which drifted between God and sports and girls and friends and school.

High school graduation brought some freedom, both in where I lived and how I chose to live my life. It also brought intellectual freedom, the chance to test my faith on its own merits and not on the foundation of my family or friends. I wondered if the spiritual kindling my parents chopped while raising me would burst into white-hot flames for Christ. Instead, it absorbed the water of the world.

The smoldering that resulted during my college years at the Air Force Academy led me off the path of faith and plunged me headfirst into a lukewarm pool. I continued to go to church and occasionally read my Bible, and all of my friends knew I was a Christian. But while I was there, I slowly began to compromise my faith, tempted by the allures of sin I had not faced in my Christian life back home. I was a head-Christian during this time, still believing in God and His principles, but my heart had wandered far from Him.

A year or two after college, I came up for a deep breath of air in God's kingdom. When I did, I was in Los Angeles as a second lieutenant, attending church on a regular basis and involved in a Bible study with my Air Force buddies. I had fallen in love with surfing, which connected me to God's creation in a whole new way. I was even serving in the church youth group and involved in homeless ministry. But as I regained my footing on my journey, breathing in the study of the Word and the glory of God's creation and exhaling acts of service and compassion, my heart only occasionally took joy in God and soon meandered back to the tepid pools of pride and complacency.

I was constantly frustrated by my own heart. I would find God, and then I would walk away. God would bring me back to Him, and I would wander off once more. I needed a leash, and like Robinson, I wished His goodness would bind me to Him like a fetter. But God seemed to let me stray from Him just far enough to remember why I loved Him in the first place.

Nothing has taught me this more than marriage. When I first met Anna at church and began to be drawn to this fascinating woman, God started to reveal deeper places in my heart that I didn't know were there. This process brought up worthy things, like a new vulnerability and emotional depth. But it also uncovered sin, like the pride of always wanting to be right, the self-righteousness of always believing I was right, and the selfishness of always demanding that I be right. Yet the sin in my marriage that is most reflective of my relationship with God is the constant wandering of my heart.

Anna captivated me in a way no one had before; I couldn't keep my eyes or mind off this woman. She frustrated me to no end but delighted my heart in every way. I would do anything for her; one smile melted my heart. It still does. But if you ask Anna how often she feels my delight in her, she will likely say, not as much as she used to. The bus of marriage has replaced the hot air balloon of dating. And as I ride this bus each day (though it's an extremely nice bus), I too easily wander from pursuing and yielding to my first love.

As I look back over my journey so far, I realize I am a comfortable Christian, one who believes in God and wants to do His will but isn't ready to truly become a fully committed disciple of Jesus. And I hate being a comfortable Christian. Because of this hatred—or my fear of staying comfortable in my faith, or simply God's mercy—my ever-present wanderings are oscillating in smaller degrees. A furrow in my path is centering my steps and revealing my cravings for Jesus. I have tried to ignore these cravings or to fill them with pleasure, self-centered pursuits, or even service and religion, but none of these have truly satisfied.

I still wander off at times to sample the fruits of sin, but God graciously brings me back to taste and see that He alone is good.[2] He has been slow to anger and rich in mercy, and He is growing within me a longing joy that is found only in Him. The deepest cravings of my soul, which have carried me faithfully along my littered path and have strengthened me to persevere in the journey, are leading me home to Him. And I want so much more of what I am finding there.

This longing, this deep-seated craving for more and more of God, is slowly consuming my life. It is a terrifying thing to desire submission to a mysteriously unpredictable God who delights in leading people in ways that upend the world. But this kind of life has an allure that I cannot ignore. I suspect you may be like me in some ways, so I want you to know that I wrote this book for you.

I cannot say it was always this way. I actually began writing this book for me. In a more innocent sense, I simply starting recording some thoughts about what God was doing in my life. But in a darker sense, a more selfish sense, I began writing this book because of what it might mean for me.

I thought that writing a book might bring me to a place I wanted to be—recognized and respected in the Christian community. I thought I might become influential in the lives of others. Lots of others.

I wanted these others—you, for example—to be encouraged in their faith. And that's a good thing. If you had asked me if I would have been happy to influence just one life for God's kingdom instead of lots of lives, I would have told you, "Of course, the numbers don't matter. It's all about how God wants to use me," which would have been somewhat true. I think I believed that, but I really wanted more.

This wanting more crept out of a deeper part of me, a yearning to experience life more fully, to take hold of the kingdom of God in a way that would have a bigger impact. And it felt like something righteous—wanting to be used by God in greater ways. But this desire turned out to lead me off the narrow path of faith and into the self-absorbing potholes of egotism.

I didn't see it for the longest time. At first, God began to guide me into some really interesting experiences and give me the courage to try some things I might not normally try on my own. And the results profoundly encouraged my faith. As I lived out these experiences and wrote them down as stories, I found thoughts spilling out of them. Each story became a fountainhead of truth that flowed through my life and onto these pages.

But my purpose in writing began to give way to the self-glory I was experiencing from the work God was doing in my life. I soon began to forget about you altogether. When I did think about you, I thought about the conversations you might have with friends and family, about how something in particular in this book met you in the place you are today and how you are grateful to me for that. In other words, I thought about how you would think about me.

But even as I thought about you thinking about me, God was faithful to remind me of just you. As I dreamed about the road of possibilities in front of me, seeing the places I might be and the people there who might have the chance to meet me, He awakened me by peeling back each layer of pride and selfishness within me, leaving tender skin, reminding me that this is no longer about me. It's about you and Him.

Even when I forgot about you, God remembered. And now is His appointed time for the three of us (actually, the five of us) to join our paths and take a short walk together. The stories you will find in this book and the people you will meet along the way are powerful testimonies to a living and active God who has an impeccable sense of timing and a grand sense of humor. You will find the thoughts and the heart of a fool, hell-bent on heaven but often going about it in all the wrong ways. But I hope you will also find the signposts of my cravings for God and search out the longings of your own heart along your journey.

May all this find your soul wanting and aching for the greater reality of being satisfied in every way by the joy of knowing and being known by Jesus.

1. Habit:

Habits Are Good
Unless They Become Our Habit

I hate to floss.

I don't think I've ever liked it. My parents must have taught me how to floss when I was a child—they are great parents. But I don't remember them doing so.

I do remember learning how to ride a bicycle on our front lawn. I also remember learning how to water-ski behind our pontoon boat. I have some recollection of learning to snow ski down the tee boxes on the golf course near our house, and I can recall learning how to jump off a diving board wearing a super-cool green and purple Speedo. My memories of learning how to read, spell, and count are clear. And I think I remember learning how to brush my teeth and comb my hair. But I don't remember learning how to floss.

Come to think of it, I had an abnormal relationship with my dentist, Dr. Avery. I knew him to be a man of the church, and he had an expansive grin, so I felt good around him, even though he wanted to stick drills and needles in my mouth. But his best attribute was his laughing gas machine.

I really loved the man for it. Nobody in his right mind likes going to the dentist, but I did.

After most checkups, he strolled into the office lobby with me in tow, waded through the towering piles of *Reader's Digest* and *Southern Living* toward my waiting mother, flashed his enormous smile, and said these beautiful words: "Chris has a cavity."

I *loved* those four words. Joy welled up inside me when I heard them because I knew I would soon be back in that office, high as a kite on laughing gas, floating in the blissful euphoria of altered hues and offbeat sounds. That was my reward for failing to brush properly, and what a reward it was. I would return to my dentist with great anticipation, and after he finished filling my latest cavity, Dr. Avery would always give me a new toothbrush and tell me to be sure to floss. I would nod my head in superficial assent. I knew it was the right thing to do because he told me time after time and my mom told me time after time, but it just seemed so rewarding not to do it.

Maybe that is why I have never liked to floss.

As I got older, I noticed a lot of things in my life mirrored my reticence toward flossing. I don't particularly like doing sit-ups or eating vegetables. I rarely clean my shower, and I'm almost certain I have never once dusted the leaves on my fake ficus tree. I know I should spend time each day in prayer and reading my Bible, but I don't do that with any regularity. I can't remember a sustained period of time in which I consistently thought of someone else first, and I don't often look for opportunities to provide for those in need.

Finally, I believe I have the world's greatest information—the gospel of Jesus Christ, a message of great news to everyone on earth, something so important that I should not rest or eat or drink anything until I have shared it with every one of those people. But I have only told a few people about it. I haven't even covered my apartment building, much less my neighborhood, city, state, or country. And if my apartment building, neighborhood, city, state, and country are still unreached for Christ, maybe you haven't told them about this gospel either. We would both acknowledge the primacy of sharing the gospel with the world, but it seems to occupy very little of our conversation.

All of this makes me wonder if we spend nearly all of our time bypassing opportunities to do the things we know we should be doing. I see evidence of this both in my spiritual walk and in the mundane duties of being a presentable human. And as I look at the lives around me, both inside and outside the church, I think I can fairly say I'm not alone. When faced with the opportunity to do something for God, we'd rather eat chips.

Why are we like this? My own attitude toward God saddens me; I am actually pretty annoyed by it. But apparently I am not saddened or annoyed enough to really do something about it.

When I begin to feel badly about myself, I often try to take solace in the Scriptures and seek comfort in the stories of the heroes of the Bible. These were ordinary men and women who did extraordinary things for God. The apostle Paul is easily one of the Bible's greatest heroes. He wrote about half of the books in the New Testament, and he is revered as one of the foundation stones of the faith, a man given over to God's Spirit in heart, mind, and soul.

I did not write half of the books in the New Testament. In fact, I didn't write any of them. I am not revered as anything in particular that I know of. But I find Paul wasn't so unlike me in some ways. In a letter he wrote to the Christians in Rome, Paul cried out in the frustration of his flesh, "I don't really understand myself, for I want to do what is right, but I don't do it. Instead, I do what I hate."[1]

This is the story of my life as well. This inclination to do wrong, or at a minimum, to do what is easy, is as natural to me as sneezing.

Often, I know the right thing to do, whether it is going to lunch with someone who needs a friend, or sharing my faith with someone who needs hope, or simply loving someone who is hard to love. But more times than not, I ignore these opportunities or come up with excuses or reasons why I shouldn't have to act on them. Sometimes I know that what I'm about to do is wrong; I even know that when I am finished doing or saying the thing I know I shouldn't do or say, I will be sorry I did it or wish I had not said it. And I do it anyway. Thinking I can get away with this kind of thing is like walking up a sheet of ice in bowling shoes; I don't have a chance of making it up to the top, but I try anyway and fall every time.

God, however, was ready to give me cleats. I found them in David Crowder's book *Praise Habit: Finding God in Sunsets and Sushi*. One particular section caught my eye.

> Years ago a friend told me that an action repeated for a minimum of 21 days is likely to become a permanent habit. So I thought I'd give it a shot…After much thought I decided that my trained response to "Hello" or "How's it going?" or "Hi" would be to salute and wink. In the beginning it was quite fun. Some pal would walk in the room and say, "What's up?" and I would raise hand over eye in quick, sharp movements and wink while responding, "Not much." *It was beauty. The internal joy it brought was overwhelming.* It was the perfect habit to form. It was quirky but legitimate. Impossible to tell if I was serious or not. The "Sunshine Sailor" is what I called it… Soon enough, before long I didn't even think about it…until one day when I saluted the convenience store clerk and realized it did nothing inside. There was no suppressed smile…nothing joyous bursting in my chest…It was habit. I had done it.

It seems for most bad habits we [form], there was never any
intentional formation…usually, destructive habits are formed
more subtly with very little thought and planning. Good habits
seem more difficult to manage…Why does it seem like the
formation must be much more intentional in our adoption of
good habits?[2]

Lacing up these cleats, I reflected on this passage, and I thought a lot about
the concept of habit forming. I often think of something that would be good
to do on a regular basis, and sometimes I try my hardest to do it. Or I may
find something about myself that I don't like, or something that someone
else doesn't like about me, and if I agree with them, I try my hardest not
to do it. I usually have some measure of success with my attempts toward
personal change, but they never seem to work out on a long-term basis.

Searching for answers, I turned to the source of all knowledge: Google.
I searched on the following phrase: "I do the things I don't want to do,"
looking for commentary on the apostle Paul's frustration with his flesh,
hoping to find some other poor soul who had felt my pain or had lived
what I was living or had experienced what I was going through and had
come out on the other side.

The first website Google listed opened with this:

Bored? Listless? Help is at hand!

Pass away the pointless hours with our list of things to do
when you're bored.

Push your eyes for an interesting light show.

Try to not think about penguins.

Repeat the same word over and over until it loses its meaning.

Try to swallow your tongue.

Step off a curb with eyes shut. Imagine it's a cliff.

Have a water drinking contest.

Stare at the back of someone's head until they turn around.

Pick up a dog so it can see things from your point of view.[3]

Let me be clear: I appreciate the creativity this represents, and if I were to be completely honest, I have to admit I am thinking of penguins right now. I also wish I had a little dog.

What bothers me, though, is this: Why did this useless information appear when I went looking for Bible verses describing the frustration I feel with the inadequacies and emptiness of my life? Why isn't the Internet full of wisdom for souls desperately seeking a greater understanding of our human condition instead of inane information that addresses none of the real problems we face in life?

Clearly, this list doesn't answer my question at all. But as I thought more and more about this list of things to do when I am bored, I realized the words I read on that page were emblematic of the things I waste my time on every day. Maybe the things I do aren't quite as useless, but they are no more valuable when weighed on the scales of eternity.

So I decided the time had come, and I would live like this no more. My habits had to change. I decided that for the next 21 days, through rain and snow, hell and high water, under no circumstances backing down, I would floss.

And floss I did.

On the first day of my experiment, I wrote out the numbers up to 21 on a green sticky note, which I stuck to the wall beside my bathroom mirror.

Every night, when I was getting ready for bed, that day's number called to me softly. So I would floss, and then I would cross off a number. And it felt great—a neat and tidy little system of accountability.

Days flew by quickly, and nighttime would find me in my bathroom, laboring with my new, minty friend in the fight against unwanted plaque. Night after night, me and my floss. Days turned into weeks, and we were still together.

The morning of the fourteenth day, I awoke and went into the bathroom to brush my teeth. I noticed I had forgotten to cross off the previous night's number, and an anxious pause came over me. Had I failed myself yet again? My confidence returned quickly, though, as I remembered that indeed, I had flossed the night before but had forgotten to mark it down. The habit was slowly taking shape.

The days continued on, and I was excited to finally be a person of good habits. All the poor habits in my life, my little grinding sins that cling to me like gum on a shoe, my idiosyncrasies that don't bother me but drive others crazy—all of these things would soon be footnotes in the chapters of my life. My horizon was clear and blue; nothing could stand in my way from being exactly the person I thought I should be. I grew more and more content with who I was, and more importantly, with the man I was becoming.

The final day of flossing arrived as quickly as the end of an all too pleasant vacation. I had emerged as the conquering hero in this trial. I didn't need to see Dr. Avery anymore, and his laughing gas machine was now a thing of the past. I had achieved resounding success in this area, putting together a DiMaggioan streak I had never before accomplished in all my life.

As I reflected on my triumph, the simplicity of it all struck me; it merely required a little determination, a little persistence, a little accountability, and a little green sticky note.

The implications were staggering. If I could master a habit of the flesh, why could I not also master a habit of the soul? I knew life to be far more than good dental hygiene. I knew God wanted me to address my lack of discipline in my Christian walk. And I felt the deeper cravings for more of God in my life. I had tried so many different things to experience God more fully, and perhaps this notion of habit forming could be a way to satisfy these longings.

I sensed a time was coming in my life when God would need me. I knew He could use my success and my good habits for His purposes in order to advance His kingdom on earth. I had practiced on something small, but I had succeeded, and God saw what I had accomplished. He knew He could count on me, and He knew I wouldn't let Him down. Every boy who plays basketball on his driveway or practices his swing in his backyard dreams that one day, during the right game and at the right time, his moment will arrive, and he will be ready for it.

However, I also knew my time of testing had only just begun. I knew of many areas in my life that needed more practice, and I was finally ready to lay them before the Lord and say, *Teach me how to do this better.*

So I sat down to write a list of good habits I would like to have in God's kingdom, behaviors and practices I knew would take me closer to the heart of Jesus and awaken my cravings for more of Him, and I came up with a really good list.

> obedience
>
> purity
>
> charity
>
> humility
>
> love
>
> prayer

I thought of others, but I figured I should start slowly. The journey of my entire life would be spent shaping and forming these habits, but I could get started on them right away.

There were my goals, simple and on paper. Just as my little green sticky note and I had scaled the rocky heights of proper dental hygiene, so too would we conquer the sins of my soul. I began my quest in earnest, brimming with the confidence and optimism that only past success can bring, energized by my ability to make things right in my life, destined to be a person of good habits.

And clean teeth.

2. Silence:

What We May Hear in the Midst of Silence

God once called my cell phone at 4:30 in the morning.

Actually, it wasn't God on the other end of the line. If it had been, and if God had caller ID, then prayer would have become a whole lot easier. But it was simply a mere human from a credit card company calling to verify some information. She must have been the conscientious type, quickly getting to one of the first items on her to-do list on the East Coast while I lazily slept in my bed three hours behind on the West Coast. And I must have sounded incredibly rude to her as I mumbled my way through my answers to her questions.

This particular morning coincided with my successes in flossing, and as I mentioned, I was turning my attention to the more important matters of the Spirit. I was on the lookout for a spiritual problem to be fixed by my little green sticky notes, so I had a moment of pause to wonder if God was trying to get a message to me.

I tend to think God is always arranging events in my life for specific purposes. This is probably an indication of either wisdom or paranoia. If I miss a plane for some reason, I assume He must want me on the next one to talk to someone about the gospel or encourage him in some way. Or if it's raining when I had planned to go surfing, He must want me to do something else with my morning.

So there I stood in my moment of pause, bare feet chilling on a cold hardwood floor, asking myself, *Why did I get this call on this morning?*

Before long, the memory of the previous night came to me, and I remembered the conversation I had wrapped up with my brother, Scott, just before I fell asleep. We talked about a lot of meaningless things, but one of the more useful topics we discussed was prayer. I told Scott about how little I prayed and how ineffective I seemed to be. I shared with him that I had always wanted to find a place of solitude to pray but had never actually done it. By the end of the conversation, we had talked about not just praying with a list and not simply telling God everything that was on our hearts, and we discussed the need for giving God ample time to reply.

In other words, we talked about praying by listening.

Here was my chance to transition my habit forming successes into the spiritual arena and to do exactly what I had confessed to Scott I had not been doing. Summoning my resolve and shaking my limbs in an attempt to wake up, I entered my walk-in closet with the hard and ugly vinyl floor, shut the door, got on my knees before a wicker laundry hamper, rested my elbows on top of a pillow, respectfully bowed my head, and proceeded to embarrass myself completely before God.

I fought off sleep the entire time, waking from an unfinished prayer several different times. I changed positions from kneeling to sitting to kneeling again because I thought sitting wasn't respectful enough. I tried talking to God quietly in my head, but my mind wandered off in many directions. I attempted to talk out loud, but I felt silly. I struggled with all my might to clear my mind and focus only on God, but I just couldn't stay engaged.

I admit I didn't even come close to my goal. As I kneeled in my closet, I questioned whether God had called me into that prayer closet in the first place and soon began to think He might be calling me back into my warm bed, and I was all too willing to follow that leading. As I stood to exit my closet, I guessed I had been in there for about 15 minutes, feeling a little guilty that this was all I could muster for God. Opening the door into my bedroom, I sheepishly shuffled back to my bed and glanced at the clock on my bedside table. Almost an hour had passed, although I suppose a good 40 minutes of it was spent in and out of sleep.

I took great comfort in the fact that I had prayed for an entire hour, although, as I mentioned, most of it probably didn't count. But it was longer than I had ever prayed before. Still, I can't say it was an enlightening time with God; in fact, I don't remember anything from that morning's prayer. All I remember is that I had to fight to be still, be awake, and listen.

Praying by listening soon became a challenge I wanted to accept. On some days I tried to do it; on others, I didn't. But I knew I could ultimately make this a regular discipline. To address my problems, I created a new sticky note and put those 21 numbers on it again, and I stuck that little green sticky note on the bookshelf in my closet. I recognized that a little discipline and accountability would help my situation, and I expected to become the man of prayer I longed to be.

The sticky note definitely made a difference: I made it three days in a row. Half of the time in my closet was spent fighting off sleep, and the other half was devoted to containing my rambling thoughts.

God, You are so amazing and majestic. The heavens declare Your glory, and there's nothing quite like a sunset to show off Your artistry. I love to watch the sun setting over the ocean, God. You know, I love the ocean. In fact, my favorite place to be is sitting on a surfboard in the water at El Porto, gazing over the mountains behind Malibu. Actually, that view is *always ruined by the smokestacks at the oil refinery. Who would put a refinery on the beach? I wonder how they actually make gasoline? You know, it cost me $60 the other day to fill up my truck. Why are gas prices so high right now?*

I shook it off.

God, I'm sorry I wandered off there. Thank You for Your mercy and for always being there for me. You are such a loving Father, and You are always so incredibly patient with me, even when I'm off doing my own thing or I'm stuck in a rut. You know, Anna was in a bad mood the other night; I said what I said to her to try and help, but it only made things worse. I don't think she was actually listening to me at all, and it was really hard to be patient with her. But I was. I'm a pretty patient guy; no, I'm a really patient guy. Don't You agree, God?

Despite three successive days of deeply spiritual prayers like these, I missed the fourth day and had to start over with a new green sticky note. The next round of attempts lasted for two days. At that point, I knew something was definitely wrong with my approach, but I decided that the problem wasn't me. The problem was simply that I was relying on a green sticky note to help instead of just being disciplined enough to pray every morning. I had a revelation: The easy solution was to continue the habit-forming process but without the green sticky note. Subsequently, the situation improved dramatically, and I made it four days in a row.

There was no 21-day victory, no Sunshine Sailor, and no prayer-time equivalent of sparkling clean teeth. Needless to say, my confidence in these little accountability partners was quickly fading, and I realized I had traded the God of the universe for a god of green sticky notes. Worst of all, my attempts to make myself into a person of spiritual habits did little to satisfy my longings for God; in fact, the cravings began to subside as I started feeling worse about myself because I couldn't do something as simple as talk to Him.

As I moved past my failures in habit forming, I turned my attention back to my prayer life, thinking long and hard about my inability to pray, my tendency to fall asleep in prayer, and my failure to spend time listening to God. In search of more guidance, I turned to the Bible rather than Google, and as I read through the Gospels, I noticed something all too familiar in the account of Jesus' night in the garden of Gethsemane.

On that particular night, just before Jesus was betrayed and arrested, He took His disciples into the garden. A heaviness filled the air as the wind stirred gently through the low limbs of the stout olive trees. In this garden, Jesus came face-to-face with the harsh reality of what He was about to endure. He would soon ask God for another way besides the cross, and He would sweat blood in His gut-wrenching anguish. This was the crucial night in the life of Jesus, His dark night of the soul.

As He went farther into the garden, He brought along His three closest disciples, and He told them to keep watch. Before leaving them to be alone, He gathered them together, sorrow filling His eyes and anguish gripping His face. As they grew silent, He agonized with them, saying, "My soul is crushed with grief to the point of death. Stay here and keep watch [stay awake] with me."[1]

He then went even deeper into the garden to pray, coming back shortly thereafter to see His disciples fast asleep. He rebuked them, encouraging them to stay awake and pray, saying, "Couldn't you watch with me even one hour? Keep watch and pray, so that you will not give in to temptation. For the spirit is willing, but the body is weak!"

Jesus again left His chagrined disciples and continued to pray, returning to find them asleep once more. After leaving them a third time to pray, He again came back and found them out cold. When He saw this, Jesus, fully resigned to His fate of solitude, told them quite simply, "Go ahead and sleep. Have your rest. But look—the time has come. The Son of Man is betrayed into the hands of sinners."

I try to imagine myself as one of His disciples on that pivotal night.

Three years earlier, this rabbi had asked me to quit my job and follow Him. I had heard He was a respected teacher, and He wanted *me* to be one of His disciples, to learn to do what He did. Something came over me—one of those moments when I had to do something or else I wouldn't be able to breathe. There was little time to say goodbye to my father and my friends; this rabbi was on the move, and the spirit of intrigue and adventure was moving my legs in His direction.

So I did it. I left my old life and began to follow Him. Before long, I saw Him turn six 30-gallon pots full of water into wine, and I thought He would be nice to have around at parties.

I heard Him say some remarkable things over the next few years. One day, when we were walking through a field on the Sabbath, we were hungry, so we started plucking off some of the heads of grain, which technically violated one of our laws about not working on the Sabbath. When the Pharisees confronted our teacher, He told them, "The Son of Man is Lord, even over the Sabbath!"[2] You should have seen their faces when He said that; it was pretty funny.

Another time, He told a synagogue full of people that they had to eat His flesh and drink His blood in order to have eternal life.[3] That one confused even us. But His most controversial claim came when we were in Jerusalem for one of the large feasts. We were walking with Jesus through the temple when the Jewish leaders started to pepper Him with questions. He began answering them by talking about His Father, and then He dropped a bomb on them by saying, "The Father and I are one."[4] These guys went into an uproar, even picking up rocks to stone Him for making Himself equal to God. We were terrified, but Jesus talked His way out of the situation, and we got out of town.

If His astonishing words weren't enough, I also saw Him perform some mind-blowing miracles. This carpenter-turned-itinerant-preacher was making blind men see, including a man who had been blind from birth. He put His hand on a leper and healed him, which was wild because most of us hadn't ever been close to a leper, much less touched one. He also fed 5000 men and their families on one occasion with only five barley loaves and two fish that a young boy gave us. And He capped off that night by walking out to us on the water. Peter even got out of the boat and walked on water too![5]

These were all amazing miracles, but even more remarkable were the dead people we hung out with. We went to one town where a local ruler approached Jesus and made a completely unreasonable request. He must not have been thinking straight because of his grief. He told Jesus his little girl had died, but if Jesus would come and lay His hand on her, she would live again. I thought maybe Jesus could have healed her illness if we had gotten there sooner, but once people are dead, they are dead. But Jesus followed the man, entered his house, and brought out a living girl. And perhaps to prove it wasn't a fluke, He did the same thing for one of our friends who had been dead for four days.[6] I had so many questions for Lazarus that night.

My memories are suddenly interrupted by a chilling breeze. I look up into the darkened sky, thinking it is even darker than usual. My mind lingers on that first day, the day I left the only life I had ever known to follow Jesus. I realize how little I had known about Him at the time. The intrigue drew me in, and a small voice inside me told me to trust this man. But as I followed Him from town to town and watched Him touch the hearts and minds of so many, I slowly began to think He might actually be who He said He was. I actually began to believe I had been traveling with the long-awaited Messiah, prophesied about and eagerly anticipated by our people for hundreds and hundreds of years.

He had been completely selfless in all things, always giving of Himself to those who wanted to be around Him. He had met the needs of others, man after man, woman after woman, child after child, never demanding to have His own needs met. And now, in this moment in the garden, during the cool stillness of night, He seems to be in need. This is my one chance to do something for Him.

And I fall asleep.

Jesus' final response to His disciples during this event is interesting. The first time He came back to them, He seemed a little dismayed, saying, "Couldn't you stay awake...even one hour?" The second time He returned must have been similar. But the third time was different. The third time, resignation was in His voice. He said, "Still asleep?"

I am saddened that He wasn't surprised by their inability to stay awake with Him. He clearly wanted something from them—the comfort of a nearby friend during a hard time, or their watchful eyes looking for the imminent arrival of His betrayer, or simply their listening ears to hear His pleas to His Father so they would identify more strongly with the immensity of His sacrifice. But though He desired something from them, He didn't seem all that surprised when they failed Him.

I wonder if Jesus isn't surprised by my inability to stay awake with Him either. After mulling over these thoughts, I went back into my prayer closet and confessed my inability to listen well and be available to Him. I began talking to Him about these struggles, asking Him about the time His disciples failed Him. I fell back into my routine of praying through ACTS (adoration, confession, thanksgiving, and supplication). I tried to think of nothing, but that only made me think of everything.

One Sunday during this ongoing struggle, I asked my pastor, Zac, if he practiced the habit of silence. He responded that he did. I explained to him that I tried to concentrate my thoughts on God, on His creation, on His qualities, or on nothingness. I told him I had trouble being silent before God, and I wasn't sure if I was doing something wrong or needed to try something else or if I was just destined for an immature prayer life.

Pastor Zac's response to me was quite simple. He said, "I think you're making this too hard. Just go and be silent before God. That's it." Sometimes the most profound truths are hidden in the simplest of answers.

So I began doing just what he told me to do. I did away with the green sticky notes for good, abandoning my quest to be a person of good habits, leaving all my past successes lying in impotence at the door of my closet. I didn't complicate the matter with elaborate plans. I just went to bed a little earlier, and I made sure I prayed at times and in positions that would be conducive to a good conversation with someone. Basically, I stopped trying so hard, and instead, I just sat still before God, open to anything that might happen.

Remembering what God did during those times is delightful. Silence brought a wellspring of thoughts, each stream cascading down the rocky paths of my life and smoothing over the rough edges of my perspectives about life and faith. As I let God direct my thoughts, I found myself dwelling on some issue or relationship or idea and working it over in my mind, processing and polishing it until I could see what to do next. And I also felt more engaged in my interactions with God, less distracted and more energized by the growth that was occurring.

I don't know that I stumbled onto any sort of spiritual secret. I think I just realized that prayer was meant to be a conversation, and I had spent all of my prayer life talking to God without ever taking the time to listen. In fact, I had talked so much that I often bored myself to sleep.

I had longed for intimacy with God for much of my life, but connecting with an inaudible and invisible Father was just so hard, particularly when I felt like a fool for talking into thin air in my darkened closet or for chasing thoughts all over creation in my head. The disciples must have had the same experience in the garden that night. After all, they didn't fall asleep when Jesus was talking to them face-to-face. They only fell asleep when He wasn't there, when they were left to engage their invisible God in prayer.

Their struggle and my struggle aren't just about falling asleep or being distracted during prayer, and they aren't about our inability to be silent. Most of our times of prayer are actually in quiet places because we often pray to God in our heads. So our issue in prayer is that we don't engage in an adequate conversation. We tend to talk at God rather than talk with Him.

So as I crave more of God, I want to have a meaningful dialogue with my heavenly Father, to enjoy more intimacy with Him than I've ever had before. And the only way I can have this kind of relationship is to keep my mouth shut at times, which is much harder than it may seem.

King David might have been thinking of this truth when he said, "Be *still* in the presence of the LORD, and wait patiently for Him to act." We see the command elsewhere in Psalms: "Be still, and know that I am God."⁷ David knew of the tremendous power in stillness, the forcefulness of perspective that overwhelms the mind and spirit with thoughts outside of itself. The roar of mental activity soon slows to a gentle murmur, and the mind's eye opens to a wider viewpoint that makes self-centered concerns seem unimportant.

I think this is why God spoke to His people in the midst of silence. Elijah heard the Lord in a gentle whisper. Samuel heard the voice of God calling to him in the stillness of sleep.[8] And Jesus would often retire to the hills alone, to be with God in the tranquility of night.

So silence makes room for God to speak, and it also makes for better conversation. After all, I can think of far more to say to someone who is talking back. And this kind of dialogue helps me cover more meaningful ground with God. The typical empty praise, where I try to think of big words I have heard in a hymn or someone else's prayer, no longer seems worthwhile. In a two-way conversation, I can get more real and talk about the sin I've been hiding and haven't wanted to deal with. And I naturally want to thank God for giving me as much as He has, including the gift of conversation with Him.

Sometimes I make time for conversations like these with God, and sometimes He speaks to me in the silence. At other times, He's silent in the silence. And sometimes I ignore Him altogether, never seeking Him out to talk. I still wish God would call me on my cell phone, and engaging with Him would still be easier if I could audibly hear His voice. But until I meet Him face-to-face, I can always kneel before my wicker laundry hamper, opening my eyes to the darkness and my ears to the silence from which God often speaks.

Because only in silence can I hear my Father's voice.

3. Window:

Being Mindful of What Sneaks Through Our Windows

The eyes are the windows to the soul.

This is one of those phrases I have heard throughout my life that sound authoritative. I don't know where I originally heard it, who first said it to me, or how many times I have said it myself. I don't think anyone taught it to me in grade school, and I don't recall hearing it in church. But I believe it because it sounds as if it must be true.

I do know that if someone came up to me and said, "The eyes are the…." the first thing I would say back would be "…windows to the soul." I would smile, and the other person would smile, because we would both feel good about knowing the same truth.

I don't often use this expression in daily conversation, but I recently saw an infomercial that reminded me of it. The product being sold was called the Twin Draft Guard, and you could get it for $19.99, although if you called in at that moment, they would send you a second one free and even throw in a very nice-looking door hanger. The Twin Draft Guard was created to prevent heat loss from your home. This "patented double-sided insulating miracle" will "minimize energy loss from doors and windows" and help you to "save BIG money on energy bills."

This product sounds like an extraordinary technological achievement, perhaps even something that NASA developed in a secret lab somewhere in Nevada. But upon further investigation, it looks to be a simple device made by two foam pieces joined by a skin of cloth, all of which you slip under a window or door that is exposed to the outside elements. It looks kind of like floaties for your window. I consider myself to be a spiritual person, so I'm intrigued by anything miraculous, and spiritual or not, I'm always interested in saving BIG money.

To be honest, the Twin Draft Guard sounds amazing. It promises to lower my heating bill by hundreds of dollars and make me indescribably happy and satisfied with my life. Anna and I live in Los Angeles right now, so our heating bill is about seven dollars a month during the winter. So if the Twin Draft Guard can lower our bill by hundreds of dollars, our gas company is going to end up owing us a lot of BIG money, which will be fantastic because Anna will be able to buy more shoes.

As I thought about the obvious financial and practical benefits of the Twin Draft Guard, I did what I normally do, which is to carry an analogy much further than it ever should go, and I began to think about the windows to my soul and to wonder if any drafts were getting in through the cracks and cooling off my fire for Jesus.[1] What if our eyes, and our ears for that matter, don't do a good job of protecting our hearts and minds from the outside elements of the world? What if things that we don't want inside are actually getting inside? And what if we're not aware of them at all?

To make this analogy airtight, we have to picture our bodies as houses. Fortunately, Paul describes us in this way when he asks, "Do you not know that your body is a temple of the Holy Spirit within you?"[2] And like a house, the inside is affected by what comes in from the outside. So anything coming in through the windows of our eyes and ears is bound to have an impact on our souls.

I spent a few days thinking about this concept of my eyes and ears acting as the windows to my soul. What have I been letting in all of these years, and has it been sucking the life out of my longings for God? What is now inside that has no business being inside? After all, a window is designed to allow certain things in, like light, and keep other things out, like bears. Some things are always better left outside.

All of these thoughts reminded me of a story my dad once told me about his tour of duty in Vietnam. He flew helicopters during the war, and he said they had a tradition for pilots who returned from their first combat mission. The other pilots threw a party, got the rookie pilot drunk, cranked up the music, and projected pornos onto a screen they had set up in camp. This was a bunch of guys at war who were trying to blow off the steam and stress of combat duty. None of them considered the way these images streaming through their eyes were damaging their souls.

Forty years have passed since my dad was in that environment. Today, he is a godly man for whom I have the utmost respect, a man who has taught and demonstrated the virtues of integrity and purity. But during the war, his windows were wide open, and the houseguests he welcomed in back then have been hiding out for years in his basement. As he continued his story, he talked about driving along in his car and hearing an oldie on the radio, a song he had heard during one of those parties in Vietnam. He said the images came screaming back into his mind. He wasn't looking for them, and he didn't want them there. They just showed up.

In effect, they were party crashers.

Nothing is worse than throwing a house party and having people show up unannounced and uninvited. In most house parties, the crashers walk right in through the front door, and often, they are either not welcome or not even familiar to the hosts. But the party crashers of sin are sometimes not so obvious, and sometimes they aren't strangers. Some sins have been at your house at least once before. And more times than not, these sins don't walk through the front door, alerting the entire house to their presence. Some crawl out of the basement, and others come in quietly through the windows.

As I considered what I had been allowing through my own windows, I began to be more intentional about letting fewer crashers into my house. Some of these crashers are images. Others are ideas I hear about life or women or money or cars. I realized these crashers were polluting my soul and robbing me of my desire for God, and I was reminded that purity—emotional, physical, mental, and spiritual purity—is a big deal. The reason it's such a big deal is that all of the images and sounds that come into our souls through our eyes and ears become a part of us and shape the men and women we are becoming.

So I decided to take inventory of what was coming in through my eyes and ears. Sometimes, my windows are wide open, and any sight or noise can come right through. Other times, they seem to be shut tight, but I wonder if small drafts of sin are slipping through the cracks without notice. Solomon seems to have been onto this idea when he wrote, "Guard your heart above all else, for it determines the course of your life."[3] Solomon could just have easily told us to get a spiritual Twin Draft Guard.

I first thought about the images I had allowed to enter through the windows of my eyes. Initially, I didn't come up with much, rationalizing that most of what I saw was through passive observation, just seeing whatever was in front of me as I lived my life. But I slowly began to realize that I subject my mind to visual toxins nearly all the time:

Magazine rows at the convenience store or the checkout aisle at the grocery store. Billboards along the highways and neighborhood roads. Commercials on every single channel. Prime-time television shows. Movies in theaters. Movies on DVDs. Internet sites—even the normal ones.

These crashers are inside my house and seared into my mind. Thousands upon thousands of pictures and billboards, layers upon layers of images and snapshots, and years upon years of toxins have slowly eaten away at the purity of my soul, rotting me from the inside out. Yet they are never quite painful enough to notice or blatant enough to respect.

This was a troubling realization. I didn't consider many of the things I look at as all that dangerous. I'm certainly not hanging out at the Playboy Mansion on Saturdays or watching reruns of Baywatch on Sunday afternoons. Most of what I see seems fairly harmless.

But God spoke to my naïveté through the story of Job (a man whom God called "blameless and upright"), which contains a remarkable conversation between Job and some of his friends.[4] In their dialogue, Job makes this comment in defense of himself: "I made a covenant with my eyes not to look lustfully at a girl."[5] Job, so intent on obeying God and maintaining his purity, made a covenant, not with God, but with himself. In this covenant, he said he would not even *look* upon a girl with lust in his heart. Jesus' words about adultery ("Anyone who looks at a woman lustfully has already committed adultery with her in his heart") confirm what God had already revealed to Job.[6]

Shortly after discovering Job's covenant with his eyes, I remembered an evening Bible study a few years back. Our group, called the Newmen, gathered each Wednesday at a church in Manhattan Beach. This group was known for its transparency and honesty, and one evening as I listened to the guys talk about trust or obedience or something spiritual, I was overwhelmed by a sense of conviction and the need to confess something to them. Interrupting the flow of the conversation, I said, "Guys, I have been thinking a lot recently about dealing with lust. I realized I have become too complacent in what I look at—girls out on the beach, sex in movies, magazine covers at the store, or sometimes even pornography. I suspect many of you guys are probably in the same boat. I just know I'm tired of it, so if you're interested in some sort of accountability, come talk to me afterward."

The room was silent, and everyone looked at me uncomfortably. Have you ever thought you really needed to say something, and you struggled with the fear of saying it, and then you finally did, and the result was not quite what you expected but instead was completely awkward? This was one of those times.

But God had something in mind for us at the time. After we finished for the night, 14 guys came up to me and gave me their e-mail addresses. We spent the next 30 days in reckless pursuit of purity in both deed and thought. Each night, I wrote an e-mail to the group to say, "God brought me success today." Each guy wrote back, telling the group how God had worked in his life that day as well. And the 30 days went well, each guy learning to make and keep a covenant with his eyes.

During that season of my life, I had firmly secured the windows of my home. Nothing got in without my knowledge. But over time, leaks began to develop again, and I failed to notice the small cracks that let in the seemingly innocuous images. I felt guilty about this, and I confessed my lack of purity to God again. And I put people and systems of accountability in place to prevent those leaks from bursting open once more.

I realize that not all that comes through the eyes is about lust. This is certainly a huge struggle for men and likely a struggle for some women as well. Even the sister sin of lust for many women, the emotional desire for a certain man or the constant comparing of the one you have to the one someone else has, is often fed through these windows. But the eyes are also portals for coveting and judgment and idolatry and greed as well.

One afternoon a few years ago, I was shopping for an engagement ring for Anna. I had decided to have a simple custom ring made for her, and I wanted to look at what was out there for some ideas. So I went to a Tiffany store in a really nice outdoor mall in Santa Monica. I hadn't been shopping in months; I'm not sure I had even been *in* a store for months except for grocery stores or drugstores. But as I walked the pathways between the shops, I was overwhelmed with a desire to start buying stuff. It didn't matter what it was—cookware, floor lamps, Xbox games (I don't own an Xbox), swim trunks, body lotion (I don't use lotion), sunglasses, a grilled sub—I *needed* it.

Fortunately, I got out of there without draining my savings account, probably due to sticker shock from my visit to Tiffany. But I was confused by this compulsive desire to spend. As I drove home, I thought about this feeling that had come over me, and what I came up with was pretty interesting. I realized I had stopped watching TV about two months before this time, and as a result, I had seen fewer advertisements. Going to this mall was my first real journey back into the visual minefield of our consumer culture. And I was immediately lured right back into it.

Beyond greed and lust, I could go on to other challenges to purity. I make judgments about others just by the way they look, or I look at people living in a really nice house and sometimes wish I had a house like theirs. But though my eyes are clearly tools to be used for evil, they are also windows to see what God is doing in the world. So these windows are useful and productive for my faith so long as they are sealed properly.

Having sought to find and fill the cracks around my eyes, I next thought about the auditory toxins I had allowed to enter through the windows of my ears. The visual toxins are certainly dangerous, but they are an obvious kind of danger, like a man standing before you with a gun pointed at your face. Other, far more subtle contaminants can slip through the windows and infiltrate the soul, and these are potentially more dangerous because they are less obvious.

One of these subversive pollutants is the noise inside my head. As a result of my experiences with prayer and my new attempts at silence, I have been trying to have a better discussion with God. This kind of dialogue with Him was difficult for me because of my constant thoughts. I am so used to thinking and processing all of the sights and sounds of our fast-paced world that even when I pause for a moment in silence, the thoughts continue to swirl like a slowly draining sink. And this makes listening to anyone, especially God, difficult.

I once worked with a woman who didn't listen. She was a whirlwind of thought and activity, thousands of strands of stress wrapped tightly in a ball of mental yarn. As I talked to her, she clearly didn't hear anything I said, and developing any sort of meaningful professional relationship with her became very difficult. The give-and-take you'd expect from an interactive dialogue just wasn't there.

I think part of the problem that plagued her was an occupied mind, much like I have during prayer. She was constantly processing thoughts, and when she was done processing a thought, she opened her mouth to release it. That thought would reach air with eager anticipation, and before that thought had dissipated, she was already processing the next thought. All this processing left little room for listening.

I cannot really fault her for this because I do it all the time. When I work really long hours, I often find my brain constantly processing all sorts of things I need to do and people I need to contact and problems I need to fix. These thoughts stay with me throughout the day and accompany me to bed. When I wake up the next morning, my mental activity hasn't stopped at all. Sometimes I try to calm my mental storm through prayer, but the noise continues to rage inside my head.

Music makes this problem even worse for me. I love music; I can do almost any menial, mind-numbing, or inconvenient task as long as I have music playing. So naturally, I play music as often as I can, whether at work or in my house or in my car. My downfall comes when I get a song stuck in my head, because it just won't go away. As I write these very words, I have Johnny Cash's "Folsom Prison Blues" in my head. I've heard the train a comin' for hours now. I cannot get rid of it. When I go to bed tonight, the song will still be in my head as a soundtrack. When I turn out the lights and lay quietly before my God, Johnny will still be there. Chances are that when I wake up tomorrow morning, Mr. Cash will be the first person to greet me.

I don't want all of this mental noise—the thoughts and the worries and the lyrics turning over and over again with no end. But I realize I have created this situation because I have welcomed far too many people into my house, and it's killing my conversation with God. My boss and the people I have to meet with tomorrow just climbed through the window into my living room and are sitting on my couch talking. Johnny Cash and Jack Johnson are already hanging out in my kitchen. Chris Tomlin just climbed through my bathroom window, and David Crowder is on my roof trying to get in. Appointments I have to make are hanging on my walls, and I've filled my bedroom with concerns about what kind of job I'm going to do next and where we're going to live.

Among this house mob, I have left so little room for the Spirit. Maybe He's hanging out in my darkened walk-in closet, waiting for me to come spend the evening with Him. Wherever He is, I certainly can't hear His gentle whisper among the din of my crowded home.

All of this noise is quietly robbing my soul of its life. Most of these thoughts or people aren't sinful in themselves. In fact, Chris Tomlin's or David Crowder's music really helps connect my spirit with God in a meaningful way. The problem occurs when the space where God speaks is filled with someone else's voice. If Satan cannot prevent me from speaking to God, his next best option is to drown out God's voice so I forget what it sounds like.

So I have had to take steps to reduce the clutter in my mind. I have to leave work at work and my concerns for my future at the front door because I need my couch and my bedroom back. I have to turn off the TV and the radio and the Internet a little more than I would like, so Chris Tomlin and Jack and Johnny are going back out the windows, and David Crowder's staying on the roof. In effect, I'm asking God to seal off the windows of my ears once more. This is a joint process, with me pressing the off button or asking God to help settle my mind while He creates the space to speak. And He has been faithful to do this when I ask for His help.

Perhaps this is one of the reasons we receive the Spirit to live within us after we have professed our faith in Christ. Personally, I have been an awful tenant. I've had parties almost every night, and crasher after crasher has slipped in through the windows to wreak havoc inside. Indecent pictures are strewn about the floor, people are in every room, and the crowd regularly keeps the clamor at a fever pitch. I've given up trying to clear out the riffraff and clean up the mess.

You may be an unpleasant tenant as well. But with the Spirit living in our houses, things like holiness and purity and righteousness become real and pressing demands on our lives. No longer are they banners to be hung from the rafters of our churches. They are friends whom we must invite into every room in our homes. And as we honor our guests, we must carefully watch what we allow to come in through our windows. After all, if our houses were built on top of dumps, we wouldn't throw our windows open during afternoon tea.

When God says, "You must consecrate yourselves and be holy, for I am holy," He is setting the bar for our spiritual growth.[7] I never really understood what holiness meant, and I just assumed it was something reserved for God and the angels who sing "Holy, holy, holy" all the time. But someone explained it to me, and it wasn't that complicated. Holiness means to be set apart, or to be free from anything that defiles us in God's sight. I think the reason holiness is so important to God is that He knows we will have clear minds and still spirits, ready for obedience to His leading, when we are set apart.

This sounds all fine and well, but my problem is that I am not holy at all. Maybe your spiritual house is a little messy too. My impurity spreads far from its roots of sexual temptation or a restless mind, branching out with broad limbs of pride, selfishness, conceit, and impatience into greedy air. I am impure in every sense of the word. What I allow in through my eyes and ears feeds this impurity and gives it strength each and every day. I do not have the power to starve this growing beast on my own.

The marvelous news for me, and likewise for you if you're in the same situation, is that my live-in Caretaker is holy. He knows how to clean up a room, to present it spotless and shining before the Father. As I acknowledge His presence in my home and His power to cleanse the filth and noise I have brought into it, and as I spend more time conversing in the closet to get His thoughts, I begin to taste the sweet fruit He has left on my table for my consumption and my joy. This fruit is "love, joy, peace, patience, kindness, goodness, faithfulness, gentleness, and self-control," and it proves to be far more enjoyable than my previous houseguests' offerings.[8]

At the end of the day, God has been gracious to alert me to the drafts that have been sucking the white-hot heat of faith out of my home. He has sealed my windows with His Spirit, and the Spirit is even doing some home-improvement projects as well. I still have windows and doors, and they are prone to leaking. But I have found my Twin Draft Guard, and He has proven to be a faithful partner in deciding what should and should not come in through my eyes and ears.

He doesn't bring us BIG money from the gas company, but He does prove to be the invaluable source that satisfies my soul's cravings.

4. Light:

Why Lights Can't Help but Shine Through Darkness

I pick up trash now.

I didn't use to do it, but now I do. I pick up trash at my house, at work, in airports, on sidewalks, in streets, and in bathrooms. In all these places, I find little bits of refuse that sit idly by. They wearily eye each passerby like a cautious puppy in a dog pound—tinged with fear but also waiting in anticipation for the man or woman who will be the one to take them home. Trash, after all, likes to be in a trash can.

This habit has become somewhat annoying because I have become a little legalistic about it, but it all started with good intentions when I moved into a new apartment in Los Angeles. My landlord had given me advance warning about all of the paper, but I hadn't paid much attention at the time. Soon enough, though, my front porch, my screen door, and the common area at our building were littered with every conceivable type of printed advertisement. Local eateries, barbershops, newspapers, nail salons—they all wanted my business, and they weren't shy about asking for it over and over again.

I felt as if the world was a funnel into which some supernatural being making six bucks an hour was tossing advertisements, and my building was at the bottom of it. All of that waste got really ridiculous. I shave my own head, and I like my work, so I don't need a barber. And I certainly don't need a place to have my nails done. You would also think if I wanted *The Los Angeles Times,* I would have ordered it by now.

The flyers, strewn across the ground outside my front door, soon began to catch my eye. They weren't put on the ground to begin with, as you might imagine. Advertisers are far too sophisticated to simply pile trash outside customers' homes. Instead, they stuff their flyers into the screen doors of every unit in the building.

But these were no ordinary flyers. They must have been rebellious and discontent because before long, they headed out on their own, jumping down from their safe screen-door perches and venturing into the unknown wilderness of concrete. They wandered aimlessly at first, headbanging in concert with the rock-and-roll of a stiff breeze, but ultimately they just decided to hang around with one another in the common area outside my door.

I began my annoying habit by picking up only the flyers I knew were my own; they were often the closest to my door. Before long, I began to notice that my neighbors had no such inclinations. I would see a neighbor's flyer one day, and it would still be there the next day. Day after day would go by, and this litter would become a fixture, having thrown off its rebellious youthfulness for the allure of settling down. These bits of trash became acquaintances, much like guys at the office whose names I can't remember. And each day, as I came home from work or school, I walked by and nodded in their direction, never wanting to stop for any length of time to talk but always good for a quick "what's up?" I ignored them for weeks until finally a thought struck me as I nodded once more in their direction.

You are the light of the world.[1]

What? What does that have to do with trash on the ground? Did being the light of the world mean I was supposed to set the trash on fire? No, that didn't make any sense, although I did set the building's dumpster on fire once, which is an entirely different story. But as I thought about that verse a little more, I soon realized I was just like my neighbors, nearly indistinguishable in behavior from them, at least in this one little way. If my neighbors left their flyers on the ground each day and just walked right on by, not willing to deal with something they knew they probably should, then how should I be different from them?

I know I'm supposed to be set apart, like being holy, and that being the light of the world is my charter for divergence from the customs and behaviors of the world. Jesus is telling me something about how to be different, how to shine for Him in a darkened culture.

So I decided to start being different from my neighbors by picking up their trash. Each day, as I walked past these flyers, I quickly bent over and picked them up. It was a small act of obedience, one that I don't think anyone ever saw. I'm pretty sure no one ever received salvation because of my actions either. But that's not the point. This was one small decision I could make each day to live differently, to be faithful to Jesus' expectation that I be a light to this world.

I draw some inspiration for this from C.S. Lewis. In *Mere Christianity,* Lewis offers this thought:

> Every time you make a choice you are turning the central part of you, the part of you that chooses, into something a little different than it was before. And taking your life as a whole, with all your innumerable choices, all your life long you are slowly turning this central thing either into a heavenly creature

or a hellish creature; either into a creature that is in harmony with God, and with other creatures, and with itself, or else into one that is in a state of war and hatred with God, and with its fellow-creatures, and with itself…Each of us at each moment is progressing to the one state or the other.[2]

If Lewis is right, then deciding to pick up trash as an act of obedience was one step in my progression of becoming a heavenly creature in harmony with God and others. This is undoubtedly a good thing, but ultimately, picking up trash is a superficial action that doesn't get at the depths of my heart. I want to be set apart and heavenly, to be a creature that craves God and gets along with myself and everyone else, but this desire doesn't seem to be backed up by my actions. I don't even like some people, including myself at times. And I know that's a reflection on the love I have for God too.

If I don't always get along with others, or even God, then evidently every day I make choices that are turning me into a hellish creature. And these choices are in conflict with my longings for more of God in my life. As I reflected on these thoughts, I was reminded of trash. I have all sorts of spiritual debris in my life, and I'm often like my neighbors, walking right on by, not willing to deal with it even though I know I should.

I thought of all the leaks through my windows and remembered how much garbage I had allowed to pile up in my home, never fully realizing what I had been letting in. As I spent time in silence, I also found more trash beyond the indecent pictures on the floor and the people and noise in every room, and some of this trash is stuff I've brought in right through the front door.

I spend my money on needless wants, things that feel like needs, without really ever considering that someone else in the world has a real need for water, food, a place to sleep, school books, medicine, or a Bible. I have a tendency to think I am better than most of the people I meet, but in fact, I know nothing about them, and if I did, I would probably find many of them to be kinder, wiser, and more genuine than me. I am also pretty self-centered, and many of the decisions I make at home, like how I want to spend my free time or whether Anna should get up and get us drinks instead of me, are largely driven by what I want rather than my consideration of others.

I could go on and on, but the bottom line is that a lot of garbage is piling up inside, and all of this behavior lies stinking on my floor. So Lewis is right; I do have hundreds of little choices to make each day, opportunity after opportunity, to either add to my dump or take away from it.

One such opportunity came to me in the airport in Denver. As I waited for my flight, I found an airline coupon I had been carrying around in my bag for more than a year. I kept it folded up in my little leather ticket holder my mom bought for me in high school. The coupon did not fit exactly; it stuck out to the side just a bit. It also had some weird sticky residue on it, and I'm not sure what it actually was. Regardless, this coupon was good for a one-way upgrade to first class, which was a pretty good deal.

As I read through the information on the coupon, I noticed it would expire soon. I was on my way to Eagle, Colorado, to go snowboarding with Anna and my aunt, uncle, and cousins. And I was tired, a condition in which I am almost guaranteed to be feeling self-centered. So I decided to cash in my coupon and enjoy a moment of luxury after a hard week at work.

Then I had that thought again: *You are the light of the world.* Dang it, this was bad timing. I really wanted to slump into a nice, cushy first-class seat and ignore everyone else on the flight. I didn't want to be a light, but I knew what Jesus wanted me to do, and I decided this might be an opportunity to make a choice to become a little less hellish and a little more heavenly.

So I walked up to the gate agent, smiled at her, and said, "Hi. Is there first-class service on this flight?"

She glanced up at me slowly. She was clearly tired. "Yes."

"Great. Is there room available?"

Another tired look. "No, but I can put you on the waiting list."

"Okay, thanks." I waited as she typed on her computer.

She glanced back up at me and said, "How would you like to pay for this?" I handed her my coupon. It was hard to hand over, not because it was sentimental to me, but because it was sticky.

As she read the coupon and began typing again, I leaned in and quietly said, "If a seat opens up, and you move me to first class, can you give the seat to someone else?" She looked back up at me blankly. "I don't really need the seat. I'd rather someone else have it. But don't tell them who gave it to them; just let it be a surprise."

At this point, her face no longer looked tired. Instead, she looked confused. She didn't really even say anything back to me. She just made a funny face that would have embarrassed her if she had seen it herself, looked at the ground, then back up at me, then back at the ground again. After a few more seconds, the situation became extremely uncomfortable, so I decided to walk away.

Before the flight boarded, she came over to inform me that airline policy did not allow for the transfer of seats between passengers, and it didn't matter because no first-class seats opened up anyway. But that was all right; I actually enjoyed the awkwardness of the experience. I find great satisfaction in doing or saying something that is completely unexpected, and I felt a little more heavenly because of my choice. You could argue that these feelings of joy were mixed with pride, and you would be right. But it was still satisfying to make a small choice that turned the part of me that chooses into a more heavenly creature. Before my onset of pride,

I did have a desire to bless someone else, to be a glimmer of light to a darkened plane.

I suppose Lewis could have made the same point he did about choosing by using this picture of being a light, that every time we make a choice, we are bringing the central part of us, the part of us that chooses, into more of the light or more of the darkness. The world we all live in is like a pitch-black room with one brilliant lamp at its center, and the only way we can know what the works of our hands are like is by bringing them underneath the light. With each choice we make, we inch either closer to the light or farther away from it.

I think this is what Paul meant when he wrote that we should "take no part in the unfruitful works of darkness, but instead expose them...when anything is exposed by the light, it becomes visible."[3] The metaphor makes sense because we can't see anything we do in the dark. But for a long time, I wondered what this light stood for, particularly since Jesus told us we are the light of the world.

I looked in the Scriptures and found passages that shed some, um, light on this question. Light and darkness are often used as metaphors for the righteous and the wicked, but the Old Testament only ascribes the term to one person, and that person is God. David says, "The LORD is my light and my salvation," and "your word [O LORD] is a lamp to my feet and a light to my path."[4] Isaiah continued these descriptions of God with prophetic words concerning the Messiah: "The people who walked in darkness have seen a great light," and "I will make you as a light for the nations, that my salvation may reach to the end of the earth."[5]

So when the apostle John calls Jesus "the light [that] has come into the world," and later says of His Father, "God is light," we aren't too surprised.[6] Even when Jesus says, "I am the light of the world," the only people who were hacked off about it were the Pharisees. But Jesus knew exactly what He was saying; He was claiming to be the promised Messiah.

Jesus' claim was a bold one, to be sure, but the truly scandalous statement was the one we have already discussed—His statement that *we* are the light of the world. Wait, if God is light, and Jesus is the light of the world, how are we also the light of the world?[7]

My brother, Scott, once told me a story that paints a picture of what being the light of the world might look like in our lives. Scott was an officer in the United States Marine Corps for five years. He was an infantry officer for two years and a Special Forces officer for two years. Then he got married, and for his final tour of duty as a Marine, he took a job as a regional recruiter working in downtown Portland, Oregon, where his wife, Tracy, was attending Reed College.

Reed has a gorgeous campus, terribly intelligent students, and a wide array of annual events and festivals, including Renn Fayre. Originally intended to honor and relive the Renaissance, Renn Fayre has morphed into something different. This is how Reed officially describes Renn Fayre:

> Currently, Renn Fayre is a campus-wide end-of-the-year festival. On the last day of classes the seniors march from the steps of the library to the registrar's office to celebrate turning in their theses and to be congratulated by the president. This thesis parade kicks off a weekend-long celebration with music, food and drink, sports, arts and crafts, and fireworks.[8]

Reed's website does not mention that Renn Fayre also incorporates a number of other less innocent traditions. Naked students paint themselves in blue and run around the campus. Raves, lit up by the burning arcs of glow sticks, saturate the night with revelry. Drinking is a given, and drugs are as common as Cheetos.

During the 2003 edition of Renn Fayre, a rumor was going around that undercover Feds were going to be on campus to bust students who were getting high, and all the students were buzzing about it. But the show went on as planned.

One of the highlights of the festival was the evening concert series, and Scott and Tracy went to one of the concerts. As they seated themselves in the audience and waited for the show to begin, the crowd continued to fill in and slowly collected itself tightly toward the stage. The energy in the crowd rumbled like growing thunder, and before long, small puffs of smoke rose like tiny clouds, accumulating into a thunderstorm of euphoria.

Seeing what was going on around him and his wife, Scott decided he was going to break through the storm and have a little fun while doing it. So he leaned over to a group of students sitting next to him who were wrapped in smoke like shawls, and said, "Just so you know, I *am* a federal officer," which was true, because he was an officer in the Marine Corps. But the students got a different message. Soon enough, word made it around to the sections around Scott and Tracy, and the smoke cleared, leaving these two Christians in an open clearing amid a forest of smoke.

I am not saying smoking will sentence you to hell, and you might want to argue that my brother should have minded his own business. However you see it, I still find this image of an open clearing to be compelling. Perhaps every Christian's life should look like this kind of open space, set among the haze of a world that desperately wants to cloud our vision with the desire for things other than God. In fact, this image is much like the pitch-black room with a single brilliant light at its center. The outer reaches of the room are murky, but the intensity of the light brings clarity of sight.

If we are lights in the world, we should stand out. Others should be able to see and taste and smell the beautifully clear air that surrounds our souls as we journey through a smog-filled world. And we understand why Jesus tells us, "Nor do people light a lamp and put it under a basket, but on a stand, and it gives light to all in the house."[9] Most people are sitting in the dark, and the Christ-followers are gathered together beneath the light, so they stand out clearly to everyone in the room.

But being a light is difficult. I just don't have the wattage, and I tend toward the darkness more often than the light. I face the teachings of Jesus and realize my natural inclination is to step away from the glow rather than toward it.

Deny myself?[10] Why would I do that? I like myself a lot, and I like to do what I feel like doing.

Turn the other cheek?[11] What? If someone hits me, I want to level him.

Give to those who ask?[12] Are you kidding me? You don't know how hard I have worked for this money, and you expect me to give it away to someone else?

With every choice in my day—spending time with God or blowing Him off, serving Anna or waiting to be served, getting upset with the guy who cut me off or letting it pass, showing respect to an undeserving coworker or talking trash behind his back, helping a friend move or sitting on my couch, offering my hand to the guy with the sign by the highway or turning my head away—I decide to step toward or away from the light of Christ. And these decisions mean everything to my faith. They either harden my heart, making me a bit more hellish, or they soften my spirit, making me a bit more heavenly.

Something about these choices is powerful; they can draw me nearer to God. Coming close to a roaring campfire makes you warm. Coming close to the brilliant light of God makes you a light as well. We are wicks, and the only way we can burn bright for Christ is to come close enough to catch His fire.

So as I stand in the glow of Christ in this great, dark room, I want to move toward Him. I want to delight myself in His Word and spend time in conversation with Him, allowing His light to illuminate all the spiritual trash in my home. My cravings for Him have to overcome my fear of exposure, and they compel me to do silly things like pick up my neighbors' trash.

But the great part about drawing close to God is that He draws close to us.[13] We may not always feel like that's true, but we have to keep taking small steps toward His light, knowing and believing that He will shine through us to the rest of this world. When we live in this spirit of awareness and anticipation, He will begin to show us all the opportunities we have to inch toward Him. We might even find ourselves picking up other people's trash, and they may ask us why we're doing it.

Shine away.

5. Comfort:

Calling All
Comfortable Christians

God hates all sinners.

This must be true, because a guy is standing on top of a soapbox, dressed in black and holding a large sign that says, "God hates all sinners." He has a microphone in front of him, and he's yelling into it, telling everyone within earshot that they need to repent because God hates sinners. I pause and consider whether I need to repent too, and because he is standing on top of a soapbox and speaking with the kind of authority that comes from being really loud, I'm tempted to accept him at his word. But then I remember something about God loving the world so much that He sent His one and only Son.

As I listen to what this man is saying, I glance around at the rest of the crowd, which consists mostly of people walking by and ignoring him. A few others linger, whispering quietly to their friends as they crack jokes at his expense, and to be honest, mocking this man would be easy. I know some people come to Jesus through gentle conversations, others come through fear of hell, and still others respond to hearing the gospel after observing the love the followers of Jesus have for one another. But I am struggling to see the part of the gospel that says God hates all sinners.

Theological differences aside, this man has some guts. He's standing right in the middle of Santa Monica's Third Street Promenade, an outdoor mall with a walking street down its center, and it's bursting at the seams with people. Just about anyone he knows—a neighbor, his boss, a high school buddy, or an ex-girlfriend—could be in that crowd, and nothing is more humiliating than doing something that feels embarrassing while people you know are watching you. As I leave this man's crowd and go about my way, I think of another fiery preacher—John the Baptist, working his whole camel's hair and locust thing—and I wonder why he's a hero of the Bible while I stand ready to mock anyone who dares to preach in public today. I know tolerance is fast becoming a virtue in our day, but is there such as a thing as being too tolerant?

I have thought about what it must be like to stand on top of a box like that and preach to a crowd. I'm a little embarrassed to admit that I have felt like doing something like that before. Occasionally, I get the sense that maybe that's what I'm supposed to do, to be less concerned about what people think and more concerned about giving everyone who can hear me a fair shot at receiving the glorious news of the gospel. But this whole thing just sounds so uncomfortable, and for a good reason: I am a comfortable Christian.

I really am, and I have just recently recognized it. And I'm bummed about this realization. I have cravings for God that tell me I want so much more from my faith. I read amazing tales of saints who have put their lives on the line for the sake of Christ, and I long to be counted among their company, but I often end up on my couch thinking about what it would be like to take a step of faith instead of actually doing anything about it.

Part of me wants to blame our society. We live in the most prosperous nation in the history of the world, and we're all used to modern comforts like soft mattresses, food whenever we want it, access to education and information, and money at the swipe of a card. Even if I were to do something crazy like double the amount of money I give away, I would still be pretty darn comfortable.

I would also like to blame my own personality—or maybe even God for making me the way He did. I am an introvert, and I would rather sit in a dark corner and read a book than talk with anyone. So if I am sitting in a bus or plane or standing beside someone on the street, and I sense God asking me to strike up a conversation with him or her, a conversation that might ultimately lead to me sharing my faith, I tend to pass on the opportunity more often than not.

But as much as I would like to blame society, my personality, or even God for my comfortable faith, I know the choice lies squarely on my shoulders. I am comfortable in my faith because I value comfort more than I do the glory of Christ. That's why a statement like "pick up your cross and follow me" hits me right in the gut. What are we supposed to do with something like that?

In the book *Crazy Love*, Francis Chan destroys the idea that it's all right to be a comfortable Christian:

> [What if Jesus] just showed up and said, "Follow me"? No explanation. No directions. You could follow Him straight up a hill to be crucified. Maybe He would lead you to another country, and you would never see your family again…Many of us believe we have…a reasonable portion of God among all the other things in our lives…But the fact is that nothing should concern us more than our relationship with God; it's about eternity, and nothing compares with that.[1]

Chan goes on to say that Christ may not call all of us to martyrdom, but He expects us to follow Him just the same. But I'm staggered by the thought of going from "on my couch thinking about what it would be like to take a step of faith" to "follow[ing] Him straight up a hill to be crucified." This is not an easy transition, and I bet it rarely happens overnight. After all, Peter denied Christ after three years of knowing Him. But he also became willing to go up a hill to be crucified after seeing the resurrected Jesus.

So this transformation can evidently occur through an encounter with the risen Christ, as in Peter's case, but it can also occur as I inch my way toward Christ, toward His bright light. This goes back to making small choices each day that require me to trust in God and that bolster courage rather than fear.

You know those times when you feel as if God might be asking you to do something, and it's just sitting there in the pit of your stomach, and you have an internal debate about whether you should do it? Perhaps the choices we make during those times, whichever way we choose, lead us to choose the same way again the next time. This is great news if we are choosing Christ over comfort, but it's troubling news otherwise. Those of us who are comfortable Christians are growing more comfortable with every decision we make that does not require us to trust God in the midst of our own fear. And that should make us all uncomfortable.

These thoughts of being uncomfortable reminded me of my encounter with the street preacher in Santa Monica. His version of the gospel was so horrible that I made a rash decision on the spot to go back to the Promenade to talk to people about God in a more constructive way. I didn't know what I was going to do, but I knew I wouldn't tell people that God hated all of them. I shared this decision with a few friends and asked if any of them wanted to go with me, but none of them seemed interested, and the whole thing just fell apart after a while. To be honest, I was too fearful to go alone, and when I couldn't find anyone to go with me, I was secretly relieved.

I shared this fear with the guys at Newmen one evening, telling them that this idea had been sitting in the pit of my stomach for years and that I had been consistently ignoring it. In a self-centered attempt to see if I was alone in this fear, I asked each guy to talk about the one thing he was most uncomfortable doing in following Christ. We went around the circle.

The first guy in the group said it was particularly hard for him to turn a normal discussion into one of spiritual matters.

The second and third guys both said it was difficult for them to share their faith with friends.

The fourth guy said it was hard for him to talk about God with coworkers.

The next five guys all said they were intimidated by having to answer questions about the Bible or the gospel.

The last guy said he found it hardest to truly connect with God in worship (which I took to mean he found it hardest to share his faith).

You undoubtedly notice the pattern here. I once read this quote from George Barna, the noted social researcher: "The typical churched believer will die without leading a single person to a lifesaving knowledge of and relationship with Jesus Christ."[2] This bothers me, as does my own fear of sharing my faith and the responses of my brothers at Newmen.

I knew that being a comfortable Christian wasn't solely about evangelism; lukewarm faith invades every aspect of our relationship with Jesus. But overcoming this fear violated my sacred space of comfort more than any idea I could conceive, and apparently I had plenty of company. So in desperate disregard for my own sense of well-being, I decided to get off the couch and take a step of faith.

I told the Newmen I was planning on going to the Promenade that Saturday to talk to people about the gospel. And then I paused for a moment, feeling all of the air being sucked out of the room in anticipation. Nerves came over me, the kind that spring up a half-second before you are about to speak, reminding you of how awkward it's going to be after you say whatever it is you're going to say. But I posed my invitation anyway: "I think it would be great for all of you to come along, so if you're interested, let me know."

No one said a word; the room was absolutely silent. Tension filled the room like spray foam in a small, confined space. This seems to happen to me a lot. After a few uncomfortable moments, someone made a comment that diverted the discussion elsewhere. Ignoring the hint, I issued the invitation for a second time. The silence grew even quieter, and again, no one volunteered. Their eyes went down to the floor to avoid contact with my own. Someone shifted in his seat. At this point, I was feeling a little flushed, and my eyes were pegged to my shoes. As the silence rolled on like never-ending waves, my heart began to sink.

Finally, like a burst of fresh air after sinking to the bottom of the sea, the voice of my friend Erik came soaring across the room. "I'll go." This was just what I needed, not because my invitation went off as I had planned (I had expected everyone to think it was a fantastic idea and join in with celebratory enthusiasm), but because it made me feel like less of a fool.

Later, that evening, I got an e-mail from my friend Jeff, who said, "I felt a tugging on my heart on the way home from Bible study, and I could not think of a reason *not* to do this. It is what we are called to do. You guys can count on me to be there." Anna said she would go as well, so we had a quorum.

This is when the fear really set in. Before, my idea was just an idea, something I could think and talk about without ever having to commit. But now others were involved. I had stood up from my couch, and there was no sitting down once more.

The question we faced at this point was *how* to go about sharing our faith. Should we just walk around and wait for people to come ask us about the hope we have in Jesus? Should we go to them and ask if they want to talk about God? Or should we get our own little soapboxes and microphones to tell the crowds that God doesn't actually hate all sinners?

Still tinged with hesitancy, I wanted to find a balance between being comfortable and uncomfortable—but not *too* uncomfortable. So I decided we would not stand on top of soapboxes; rather, we would sit on them. More precisely, we would take some folding chairs with us, set them up in a conversational setting, and invite people to talk to us if they were interested. I thought that the best way to invite them would be through the use of signs, so I worked through different ideas for a few days, praying over them and trying to find the perfect invitation. On Friday, the day before we were set to go to the Promenade, I came up with this:

> If you'd like to have a meaningful conversation—about God, life, love, religion, purpose, your passions and interests, relationships, money, right and wrong, heaven, hell, politics…anything that is meaningful to you—we're here to listen and talk.

My plan was to have this sentence printed on a large placard that we could set up beside our chairs. I was really excited about it; I thought it perfectly captured the right ingredients for a constructive dialogue about God. It had the word *conversation,* which is so much more inviting than *lecture.* It talked about important matters of spirituality, like God, love, religion, heaven, and hell. It was socially current, offering air time for subjects like politics and personal interests. And it had the magic word that would awake a sleeping heathen population from the mindless drudgery of their lives: *meaningful.* So I shared this idea with Anna over dinner that evening and asked her what she thought of it.

"I think it's lame," she said.

My wife has a way with words. I don't know why I had not seen it until then, but it was kind of lame. She said it was really long and people might be put off by the whole "meaningful conversation" bit, as if they had never had a meaningful conversation before with someone else, or as if I presumed they would consider a conversation with some guy sitting in the middle of the street on the folding chair to be the highlight of their week. She suggested I come up with something simpler, something that would invite people to be open to talking about God in a way that was comfortable for them.

So I scrapped the previous plans and spent several hours at Kinko's the following morning putting together a series of new signs. I had the signs printed and headed over to church to pick up some folding chairs. The time had come; I was so busy running around that I didn't have much time to be nervous. I picked up Anna and Jeff and headed toward Santa Monica. Erik planned to meet us there.

As we drove west on I-10 toward Santa Monica, I finally had the chance to consider what we were doing, and that is when the fear pounced once more. Feeling the burden of responsibility for this outing, I tried to pull myself together. Feigning confidence, I asked Anna and Jeff how they were feeling. Jeff said he was pretty nervous but was glad he was doing it. Anna said she was scared out of her mind and had no idea what she was going to say to these people. I secretly shared her sentiments.

We were about to join the circus, becoming one of *those* people, people I see on the street doing weird things. I didn't consider this behavior as "weirdness for the glory of Christ" but rather "weirdness that I hope no one I know sees me doing."

But turning back wasn't an option, so we proceeded onward. As we approached the Promenade, I drove up and down several cross streets to get a feel for the best spot to set up. The·place was overflowing with people walking up and down the street. They were moving in and out of shops and restaurants, packed tightly like sheep in a pen. We parked my truck in a parking garage, sat there for a moment, and decided we should pray. We felt as if we were in the calm before a storm because we knew that once we were done praying, the show was on.

At this point, I thought about bailing on the whole idea. Maybe we could just go catch a movie or have dinner instead. If I had been there alone, I might have done just that. But three other people were there, people who presumably had been called by God to be out there on that particular night, and I was the idiot who had suggested it to them.

We gathered our signs and folding chairs and headed for the elevators, clanking metal along the way like a Salvation Army volunteer with a Christmas bell. Once at the bottom of the parking garage, we turned our sights and our steps to the Promenade. I felt every eye watching us as we walked awkwardly along with hands full of chairs and signs, and as I was fully aware of the fact that we were there to do something strange, I assumed everyone else knew it too. Only a special kind of person can be completely self-absorbed right before sharing the gospel with someone, but I was that kind of person.

We soon found our set-up spot on the circus floor tucked warmly between two street performers: a break-dancing troupe and an amateur singer who fashioned herself as a pre-K-Fed Britney Spears. This spot had its benefits; not only was there a booming soundtrack to our conversations, but a huge crowd was gathering around the street performers and, subsequently, us.

We set up a single chair in three separate locations, and we set two chairs facing each single chair in an attempt to construct a cozy little conversation environment. We then set the three signs down on the ground on the backside of the two chairs. Anna situated herself in front of "Confess your sins." Jeff took his place in front of "What is your prayer request?" And I sat down confidently in front of "Ask anything about God."

There we sat, all by ourselves, for the longest five minutes of my life.

People poured around us like a river around a rock. Some stared, some smirked, and a few chattered. But mostly we were ignored. I quickly abandoned any confidence I was feeling and drowned myself completely in the fear that we would sit there all night by ourselves and that Anna and Jeff would hold me responsible and would never again want to talk to people about God.

My vision narrowed as the darkening fear overtook my mind. I became less aware of what was going on around me as I sank further into the depths of anxiety; all I could see was the empty chair before me. Just before I succumbed to the pressing waters, a man walked up to me and said "Hey. So...um, what does God mean to you?" My gaze met his eyes, and I buoyed to the surface, finally able to notice what was going on around me once more. Seconds later, I saw a man sit down in front of Anna and begin talking to her. A few minutes after that, a man pulled up a chair in front of Jeff.

Our confidence grew as the conversations progressed, and more people began stopping by to talk. When a chair opened up, it only sat empty for a few moments before being filled once more. On and on it went like that, man after man, woman after woman, group after group, for the next three and a half hours. We listened and talked with men, women, white, black, Indian, Hispanic, Asian, old, young, homeless, rich, educated, not-as-educated—all genuine people who were interested in talking about God. Some wanted to debate, but most of the people just wanted to have a conversation, ask some questions, listen to our perspectives, and share some thoughts of their own. A number of folks said that never before in their lives had they had real dialogues like that with Christians.

The conversations now escape me, but I do remember the joy I felt after a few hours. The fear vanished like a shadow under a spotlight, and I didn't realize until much later how comfortable I felt sitting in that chair. This was life-altering fun, enjoying heart-level conversations with perfect strangers in the middle of a surface-level environment. At one point, Anna came over to me and said, "This is so easy! Why aren't we doing this every week?"

We ended shortly before midnight, packed up our signs and chairs, and floated back to the car, this time with less anxiety about the stares. We met up with Erik, who had spent the night walking around and had caught up with a homeless guy he had met once before, and as we drove home, we all had the chance to talk through our feelings about what had taken place. Something special happened to us that night; the ice of our fears had melted in the dazzling heat of our obedience. We each had our own unique experiences, but we were collectively moved by God's faithfulness to comfort us in the midst of our fear.

That was the interesting thing about the experience. It felt so uncomfortable at first, and just showing up felt like scaling an enormous wall. But after making it over to the other side, we felt right at home, feeling comfortable in our folding chairs and in our conversations.

Since that time, we have gone back to the Promenade six or seven times. I think about 15 of my friends have now made the trip. I even went once by myself, and it wasn't that scary. Sure, I was still a little nervous anytime I struck up a conversation with someone, but it wasn't anything like the first night. I think that is part of God's blessing. When Jesus asks us to follow Him, we find He is not only leading us but also right by our side as we take each step. And we're not likely to feel scared when the Lord of the universe has our backs like that.

Interestingly, we all stopped going after about nine months; the trips just got lost in the midst of our busy lives. And when I think about starting them up again, I find the fear has crept back once more. So from time to time, I revisit my thoughts from that first night, trying to tap into the courage I once felt and the joy I had at the time. And the one thought that has lasted through time is a simple one Erik shared that night.

He said he loved the idea of going to a place where he and his wife might normally go on a date, like a mall or restaurant or store, not with the thought of being entertained but rather with the thought of being available to God. By going to the Promenade that night, we were all intentional about being there to minister to people. This is a mind-set I don't typically have, an awareness that every part of our day and every place we go are sacred. I can serve God and look for opportunities to love others every moment of every day and not just when I am "doing ministry."

I can't go to the Promenade every day with my sign and my chair. But I can take that same mind-set to my home or my neighborhood or my office, making myself available for His use and looking for opportunities to advance His work. So this is the question I have to continually wrestle with in my battle against comfortable Christianity: How do I bring the intentionality of that night to my typical day?

The answer to this question requires a huge shift in perspective. To live life like this, we must understand that our lives are not about us at all; they are about God and other people. This makes sense to me in light of Paul's stinging statement: "You are not your own, for you were bought with a price."[3] If our lives are not our own, then they belong to Someone else and therefore to many someone elses.

But I struggle every day with giving my life in service to God and other people. I am far more likely to act in my own self-interest, to meet my own needs without fully considering the needs of others. I think this is how I became so comfortable in the first place, thinking primarily about myself and making decisions that maximize my own security.

If you are anything like me, you know exactly what I'm talking about. You've settled for comfort rather than Christ, but your cravings for God are slowly thawing your cold heart. The only remedy I can see for our comfortable Christianity is to do what Paul told us, to offer our bodies as living sacrifices to a God who is worthy to receive them.[4]

So Jesus is speaking to all of us comfortable Christians, asking us to get off our couches and follow Him, to lay ourselves on the altar of life for His sake. He may indeed lead us down a path of martyrdom, or He may lead us into the heart of the inner city to care for the brokenhearted, or He may lead us into the living room of the rich to speak truth into their empty lives. He may even lead you or me to step up on top of a soapbox one day to preach the gospel.

But if we find ourselves there, feeling alone on the stage, rest assured He will be there beside us, filling us with the comfort that passes all understanding.

6. Pager:

Why We Must Always Answer Our Pagers

I sat down in 9C beside a young girl.

I could tell she was young; I thought she looked 17 or maybe a young 18. She had blond hair, a ponytail, and a curtain of bangs that covered only her right eye, like Violet in *The Incredibles.* She wore a black elastic choker necklace and pink jelly bracelets. Her red nail polish was chipped, but I think it may have been on purpose. The back of her shirt said "Purrfect" in silver, and headphones slithered their way around her head, following a black, snaked line into a CD player covered in pastel-blue sparkles.

I don't talk to people much on airplanes unless they make the first gesture. As much as I like to lead with "How's your soul?" in conversation, complete strangers don't take too well to this as an introduction. So I lost myself in *Blue Like Jazz,* the book I was reading at the time, and paid her little attention for most of the flight. Until…

Until she began writing in a little pink journal with a big, fat green Crayola marker. I couldn't keep myself from looking, peeking cautiously out of the side of my eyes, ignoring the guilt that soon came as I continued to read.

I know you are not supposed to read over people's shoulders, and you are definitely not supposed to read someone's journal, particularly a girl's journal, and even worse, a young girl's journal.

But there they were: big, green letters in a little pink notebook on a tray table in 9B. It's not like I snuck into her sock drawer, picked the journal's lock, and secretly flipped through it while she was in the bathroom; it was just sitting there in the open for anyone in 9A or 9C to see. She would write a bit, taking great care to loop the letters just right, as if the shape of the words evoked as much meaning as the words themselves, and then she would sit back and think, lost in her music. I couldn't hear what band she was listening to, but I bet it was the Cure.

Here is how her journal entry began: Chloe ♥s AJ.

That was all. Chloe hearts AJ. This was my first reaction: *No, Chloe doesn't heart AJ. Chloe can't possibly heart AJ because she's way too young, and people who heart each other for real, like God hearts us, don't write it with a big, fat green Crayola marker in a little, pink journal.* I don't know why I thought I was an expert on love, or how I had any business making judgments about this girl's love life, but apparently I thought I did.

She then flipped the page over and began writing again, very deliberately, very slowly, sometimes pausing to fill in letters with the marker or to make a small heart over each *i*.

> I gave you a second chance and you didn't take it. You don't know what you're missing out on. I was carrying our relation-ship. Where were you?

At this point, I was definitely thinking Chloe doesn't heart AJ, or at least AJ doesn't heart Chloe anymore. Her words, so childlike in their font and color, were filled with the questions and pain of adultlike grief.

You just used me to get close to her. You already had her wrapped around your finger and you knew it.

Look, I already said I felt bad about reading her journal. But I have to tell you, at that moment, I felt like I was supposed to be reading it for some reason. It was so *there,* right in front of me, almost as if she wanted me to read it. It no longer felt like a journal to be read by flashlight under midnight covers; it felt like a play to be shared with the masses. The act went on.

Anyone. Anyone at all, just please come and save me.

This was the point where I began to move from feeling that I was backstage peering through the curtains to feeling that God knew since the dawn of time that I would be front row and center in 9C and this girl would be on stage in 9B. "Anyone at all, just please come and save me." I was shouting "Jesus saves!" in my head, hoping for some sort of auditory osmosis, but it wasn't working. And then, as if that weren't personal enough, she continued.

I have so much pain that I'm just holding on. I try to get away but everywhere I go my problems always catch up. I'm so lost in this world. Why can't someone save me?

Remember, this was in green, Crayola marker. These words should have been written in blood. Her words were raw, something I would probably never be honest enough to write, and certainly not something I would write in a little, pink journal on a middle-seat tray table. Finally, the scene reached its climax.

Only one way out. It won't hurt me, but it will others…

With that, the curtains closed as she sat back and stared upward in contemplation, lost in her music and pain. I sat there, pretending to read my book, becoming more aware of the mounting call rising from the depths of my spirit, thinking, *What can I do here? God, I'm here. I'm available. Do I say something to her? Do I ask her how she's feeling? Do I take her green Crayola marker out of her hand and write the word "Jesus" beside "Why can't someone save me?" What do I do?*

So I did what any confident, bold Christian would have done: I pulled out another Christian book, not thinking *Blue Like Jazz* sounded evangelistic enough from its title, and I put it on my lap.

And I turned the binding of the book toward her just in case she might see the title, *The Jesus I Never Knew*, in sparkling gold letters and turn to me with breathless anticipation in her Bambi eyes and say, "Oh please, sir, tell me about this Jesus you never knew." I confess I was ashamed of myself at that moment. That was all I could muster, all I was willing to do for Jesus because I was too scared of bothering this girl, or sounding weird, or making her think I was hitting on her, or because I was just too lazy. So I put the book back into my bag and began to think.

Not being one to wallow too long in my failure, I soon came up with another plan. I did not feel "called" to say something to her, so I decided I would write something, because nothing quite says, "I care about you, and Jesus does too," than a handwritten note from an airplane-seat stalker who is too scared to talk to you. What I would write, I did not know, and how I would get it to her, I could not conceive. But I knew it was a great plan.

The most convenient way to execute this plan would have been to stick the note in her bag, where she kept her journal. That way, she would find the note long after I had left the plane, and I would not have to actually say anything to her at all. The only problem with this plan was that her bag was sitting right at her feet, and I think she would have noticed if I had started to dig around in it. Even if she didn't notice, surely the guy in 9A would. And the only thing worse than sticking a note in some young girl's bag while she is watching you is sticking a note in some young girl's bag while she is *not* watching you and another guy *is* watching you.

Plan A quickly turned into Plan B, which morphed into Plan C, and so on until I had exhausted the limits of the English alphabet. I was paralyzed by the multitude of options before me, and all of it was pretense anyway as I lacked the courage to do any of them.

Just as I resigned myself to my indecision, my paralysis was reversed as I noticed movement off to my left. First, the unbuckling of the seat belt, quickly followed by the stirring of the legs. This was the universal signal for all airline passengers who need to get up but are stuck behind the guy in the aisle seat. She was getting up to go to the bathroom.

She's getting up to go to the bathroom!

God was clearly opening doors; He's so good with timing. There was still one problem, though: the guy in 9A who would be watching me stick a note in some young girl's bag. But wait—he was unbuckling too. He was getting up as well. *Hallelujah!*

I quickly settled on Plan C: the business card. As soon as they had both left their seats and I had returned to mine, I pulled out a card, turned it over, and began to scribble furiously on the back.

> I'm sorry because I know it's not nice to read someone else's journal, but I couldn't help but notice what you were writing.

I glanced quickly toward the bathroom's accordion door; she was still inside. I wrote faster.

> And I want you to know that Jesus loves you and can save you.

I glanced again. The door remained quietly shut, and the 9A guy was loitering by the door, looking into the first-class cabin. This was going to work, I just knew it.

> If you'd like to know how, you can e-mail me or call me.
> Chris

The burning in my forearm reached its crescendo as I signed my name, and joyful music accompanied me as I bent down toward her bag, stealing one last glance at the door. That's when the accordion sprung to life, and out walked the bag's owner. Our seats were only two rows deep, so I knew I would be caught if I went for it. This wasn't going to work out as I had planned.

I stood back up to let her in, wondering if I could shove the card in her back pocket, but I decided that would be even worse than violating the privacy of her bag. So I stuck the card in my own pocket, feeling a bit led on by God and wondering what I was supposed to do next. After the other guy returned to our row and Chloe and I stood up to let him pass, I thought again about how I could sneak this card into her bag as he went by, but I could not find a good moment to do it.

My problems were soon compounded as we began our descent to land. Time was slipping away, and I still didn't know what to do. I glanced over at her and noticed she was looking out the window. So I started praying: *God, if you really want me to talk to her, I will. Just have her look over at me…right now.*

Nothing. No movement. God evidently hadn't passed along my message to her. Instead, He turned to me and said, *I have something else in mind.*

Okay, God. I'm serious, I prayed. *I'll really talk to her if you want. Just have her look now.*

She was still looking out the window. God spoke up once more, and again, His message was to me and not her: *Get on your soapbox.*

But I didn't want to get on my soapbox. I wanted to pretend I was willing to obey God without actually having to do it. So I tried negotiating with Him a few more times before giving up on issuing orders to God. I concluded He obviously did not want me to talk to this girl, because I gave Him a chance to show me a sign, and He hadn't, so I had done my part. It was on Him.

I went back to reading *Blue Like Jazz,* and I found myself reading a page where Donald Miller began describing when he first had feelings for Jesus. As I read his words, I went back to thinking that God had not lived up to His part with this girl. I continued to read, though, and soon the thought struck me: *This is exactly what this girl needs to hear.*

With no other explanation save God's grace, my fear disappeared immediately, and I climbed atop my spiritual perch. "Hi. Will you do me a favor? Will you read these two pages of this book? I know it's kind of an unusual request, but I just feel like you should read these two pages."

She smiled awkwardly and said, "Sure." The melancholy faded from her eyes as she took the book into her lap, and I started taking back all the things I had said to God. I realized I had no business giving Him orders; perhaps I shouldn't expect Him to do things my way.

There was one final problem though. I gave her the book shortly before we had landed, and at this point, we were taxiing to the terminal. I was watching her read out of the corner of my eye, which of course I had gotten very good at through the course of the flight, and I could tell that she was reading slowly. I made some quick mental calculations and realized she wasn't going to finish the two pages before we arrived at our gate. So I prayed, asking God to miraculously give her speed-reading skills.

And God showed up—in His own way of course.

Suddenly, the plane came to a halt. The captain picked up the mike and boomed, "Ladies and gentlemen, another plane is sitting in our gate, so we're going to have to wait about five minutes for them to push back before we can get in there. Thank you for your patience." Imagine that— God stopped a whole plane just for this girl.

As remarkable as this story was for me, I do not know its end. I did start talking to her after she finished those two pages, and I found out she was 12, not 18, and her parents were divorced, and she had just returned from visiting her father and stepsister in California and had been very lonely there. I gave her *Blue Like Jazz* and have continued to pray for her.

This is a story of fear and longing and shame and obedience, but ultimately, it's a story of a calling from God to do something He wanted me to do. You may identify with different parts of my experience as you consider what you would have done had you been in my seat. Perhaps you would have been friendly enough to say hi to Chloe from the start, easing into a casual conversation. Maybe you would have been bold enough to respond to God's leadings when they came to you instead of arguing with Him the way I did. Or you might have ignored the situation entirely and paid no attention to her.

You may relate to my fear or my reluctant obedience, but I cannot help but think back on Erik's lesson of being available to God. This has been a struggle for me, to open my day's schedule to God and to put myself into a position to hear Him when He calls. I thought more about the latter, knowing that moments of silence have, at times, brought direction from Him, but also knowing I rarely have time for silence throughout a busy day. I wondered how many times He has tried to reach me as I have gone about my day worrying about myself.

As I thought about being available to God throughout the day, my mind soon went to those doctors who are on call at all hours of the day and night because they never know when they may be needed. Their pagers could go off right as they sit down to eat breakfast, or as they leave the office for lunch, or as they settle into their couch at night, or maybe even as they take a seat on an airplane next to a young girl.

I am not a doctor, and I certainly don't have a pager; in fact, I didn't think pagers even existed anymore until recently. My friend Jordan is married to a lovely woman named Mindy, who just so happens to be a doctor. So I asked Mindy if she carries a pager, and she said she does, which is great news for this analogy.

I bet that if I were Mindy, sometimes that stupid pager would go off and I would not want to answer it. I would have just taken my seat for dinner, or just climbed into bed, or just finished a long, hard day, and all I would want to do would be to watch *The Dog Whisperer* and fall asleep on the couch. I would wonder who might be calling, or where they were calling from, or what I might have to do if I answered. But this little gadget would be beeping away at me, representing some emergency or someone who needed help. And as much as I would not want to answer it, I suppose I eventually would, because Mindy does every time.

Come to think of it, I do have my own pager of sorts. It's this feeling I get in my gut when I pass a homeless man on the street or talk with someone with whom I know I should share the gospel or ponder committing some sin I have repented for hundreds of times. I can think of any number of times my internal pager has gone off as I drove past a guy on the freeway exit or as I sat in silence beside my single-serving friend on some flight, and I have ignored it each time. In fact, my pager went off for most of my flight with Chloe, and I did my best to ignore the call for as long as I could.

You have heard the beeping of a pager before, and I'm sure you can imagine how the sound would grow fainter as you walked away from it.

Scientists who study the property of sound waves call this the Principle of Dissipation of Sound Waves As You Get Farther Away from a Pager. The funny thing about my pager, however, is that it gets louder, or stronger, the more I walk away from the situation. It tugs me back, beeping steadily, echoing against the walls of my soul. The call is powerful but not demanding, inviting but not domineering.

My pager is the Holy Spirit, and He is the megaphone for my cravings for God. The longings I feel for Jesus in the depth of my soul are amplified through the Spirit's quiet voice, and He speaks to me out of these yearnings more often than I am willing to admit. Like a doctor's pager with specific codes for certain situations, the Spirit gives me directions to follow, drawing me toward the emergencies of this world so desperate for hands of healing.

I suppose part of the reason I try to ignore His directions so often is that I don't fully understand who He is in the first place. And because I don't understand Him, I probably don't fully trust Him either. Does He really speak to me and live inside me? Or is that just an expression people use, like tapping the chest of a young boy whose mother just died and telling him she will always be with him inside his heart?

Jesus had something really interesting to say about the Spirit on the night before He was crucified. As He gathered with His closest friends for one last meal, He was surely sobered by the moment, a cloud of dread lurking quietly behind the smiles. He knew He didn't have long, and He had more words to say than time to say them. But even as He reflected on the years they had spent together, growing in intimacy and seeing God work in amazing ways in their lives, He knew that by going away, He was doing something that would be good for them. "It is for your good that I am going away," He said. "Unless I go away, the Counselor will not come to you; *but if I go,* I will send him to you."[1]

Jesus believed something was special, something was very important about this Holy Spirit, because He said the Spirit's arrival was worth His own departure.

Unfortunately, I struggle to hold the Spirit in the same regard as did Jesus. Part of the problem is that I just can't picture Him. I know that "faith is... the conviction of things not seen," and I have never laid eyes on God the Father or Jesus.[2] But I can picture them both. I imagine God as a vigorous old man sitting on a golden throne with white hair cascading down alongside a shimmering white beard, a powerful scepter in His hand, and earth as His footstool. I picture Jesus with the flowing hair and well-kept beard, lean and mean but with gentle eyes. But the Spirit is different; I don't have a good mental image of this third person of the Trinity.

These pictures of the Father and the Son are ridiculous, of course. The Bible teaches us clearly that God is spirit and does not have form in the same manner as we do, and Jesus may not have been as good-looking as the movies, flannelgraphs, or Jehovah's Witnesses' magazines want us to believe.[3] But the simple fact that I can picture them in some form seems to make it easier to relate to them.

Because I have not related much to the Spirit, and because I cannot picture Him as clearly as I can God the Father and Jesus, I did what I assume a lot of other Christians have done: I relegated Him to third best. I thought of the Spirit like a watch I had not seen in years—its alarm went off at the same time every day, but still it sat in the bottom of a drawer. I knew the Spirit was there, and I heard Him on occasion, and if I had to find Him, I probably could have, but He was not on display.

But the Spirit deserves far more than third-place recognition. He has the same prominence of deity as the Father and the Son. The three persons of the Trinity have lived forever, creating and sustaining the universe, sharing limitless power, knowing everything, and existing everywhere.[4] Even though the three persons in the Trinity are separated by position and role, God retains His internal equality and unity.

The Father is God. Jesus is God. The Spirit is God.

The fact that the Spirit is the third in a line of God's progressive revelation to mankind does nothing to diminish His importance; if anything, it demonstrates the utter relevance of His presence today.[5] When we realize He is God of the same essence as the Father and the Son, and we understand He lives within us as Christians, we're confronted by the need to acknowledge our relationship with Him in light of this soul-level intimacy. I would never treat a houseguest with the same lack of regard I often show for the Spirit.

The point in all of this isn't to fully understand the Spirit. It's simply to recognize that He has occupied far too little a place in my life.

I understand He is not a pager, an alarm clock, a megaphone, or a forgotten watch, but these images remind me that He speaks to me. I have given up trying to picture Him, but He is slowly becoming more real in my life. God's Spirit, the Spirit of Jesus, the Holy Spirit, is living within me here and now, and His presence in my life communicates one thing above all others: I ♥ you.

This is the kind of love that Chloe and AJ could not have for each other, and it's the kind of love you and I so desperately desire. So when the Spirit speaks to us, as He did to me that day on the plane, or as He did that afternoon when you saw that person in need, we don't have to fear His words.

Just like Dr. Mindy, all we have to do is answer.

7. Extra:

Why Extras Inherit the Kingdom of God

I don't like people all that much.

This isn't the best way to begin a chapter of any book being read by people, and it's certainly not something you would expect in a book about Christian faith. When I speak of my cravings for more of God, wanting Him to permeate every aspect of my life with His kind of love, I should follow that by saying I want to love others. I know just as well as you that Jesus told us to love God and love others as ourselves, but I seem to be falling way short in this area.[1] And as long as I'm being honest, let me tell you about some of the people I don't like.

I don't like people who are better looking than me, like people on TV and in magazines, because they make me more self-conscious than I would like to be.

I don't like people who are smarter than me, like the kids who got the best grades without ever studying, because they make me feel at a disadvantage in life.

I don't like people who are disciplined in diet and exercise, like triathletes, because they remind me of my own lack of discipline in those areas.

I don't like people who are really effective communicators, like compelling young pastors or speakers, because I would love to be one, but I realize I'm not.

I don't like people who are resolutely passionate about whatever it is they are passionate about, like a woman I recently saw in the airport doing yoga, completely oblivious to the awkwardness of doing yoga in front of a hundred people in an airport of all places. People like her remind me of my own lack of passion.

Before I come off sounding like I have low self-esteem, you should also know that some of the people I don't like are less attractive, intelligent, disciplined, effective, or passionate than me. This feeling is most pronounced when I see a large group of these people, whether at a concert or an airport or a really crowded street. Sometimes I survey the sea of people before me, and I assume most of them are working at jobs they don't really like or going home to husbands or wives that don't love them that much anymore. The pity you might expect me to feel is actually disdain.

It makes sense that I would try to denigrate those above me in life's ladder, because in pulling them down, I become more significant in my own mind. And while slightly less obvious, I could also have reasons to judge those I deem further down the ladder. The end result is that I believe I am more valuable than they are, as if my purpose in life is far more important than theirs.

The reason I don't like all these kinds of people seems to be not who they are, but rather how they make me feel about myself. Not liking people makes me feel significant, and I like feeling significant. Of course, this is a terribly judgmental way of viewing others and has no place in the Christian life. And it's all a lie anyway; no judgments I make of others have any bearing on their value, and feeling important in my own mind doesn't actually make me any more important.

So I take back what I said. It's not that I don't like people; I like most of the people I get to know, and I'm even coming to love many of them. I suppose the people I don't like are actually the ones I don't know, the ones I can create in my mind for my own purposes. And what I don't like is not who they are but the way they make me feel.

I wonder if I am alone in these dreadful thoughts, or if you ever find yourself doing this too—judging others in order to make yourself feel important. It's alluring and almost natural because we all want to feel good about ourselves, and being a critic is a surefire way to make much of ourselves in our own minds. But Jesus has harsh words for us: "Why do you see the speck that is in your brother's eye, but do not notice the log that is in your own eye?"[2] He also says, "Judge not, that you be not judged," and "The last will be first, and the first last," and all sorts of other things that are devastating to my own sense of importance.[3]

My own attitude bothers me because I know I should love all the people I like to judge. After all, Jesus loves them. The book of Mark tells us, when "Jesus saw a great crowd…He was moved with compassion for them," and we see accounts all throughout the Gospels of His love for all kinds of people.[4]

I've tried to produce this kind of love on my own, and I'm sure you have as well. We know we're supposed to love others, and sometimes if we don't feel like it, we will just fake loving them in hope that we actually will grow to love them. But many other times we don't feel like loving someone, and we just go with it.

One of the things that helps me want to love people is to think of their stories. Have you ever walked by strangers on the street or in a store and had a momentary thought about what their lives may be like? These people whom you do not know have parents, childhood memories, families, friends, and interests just as you do. When I realize these people have their own stories, I can't dismiss them quite so easily. I remember that their story is no less valuable than my own, that ultimately we're all part of God's story.

And here's the thing about God's story: It's the only one that matters.

Yet I am still plagued with an entirely wrong perspective on God's story. I fancy myself as one of the stars, sitting in my cushy dressing room, quietly preparing for the call to the big stage. I see God moving in my life and working His will through me, and I begin to think I am one of the chosen few who will do great things for the Lord. I lose all sense of a historical perspective on the untold hundreds of thousands of saints who have gone before me as well as a global perspective on the untold hundreds of thousands of saints who are carrying out God's mission in the world today.

When put into God's global and historical perspective, I am no longer the star I fancy myself to be. I am simply an extra.

What right does one extra in a movie have to look at another extra in the same movie and say, "My part is better than your part"? That would be ridiculous; extras are there to complete the story, not carry it. So I am trying not to be that kind of extra. I would rather be the extra who is simply stoked out of his mind to be in the movie at all.

Louie Giglio tells a funny story that has fueled my perspective on being an extra. He and his wife went to a movie one day, and after they bought their tickets and got their food and drinks, they walked into the theater, which was nearly empty at the time. They took their seats in the middle of the center section and waited patiently for the movie to begin.

Before long, Louie started to notice a pair of eyes staring at them. A guy who was sitting a couple of rows in front of them had turned his body all the way around in his seat and was looking directly at them. The guy didn't glance away and then back again as you and I might do when we're caught looking at someone. He just looked at them with unwavering focus as if they were having a staring contest.

Louie began to get that awkward feeling you might have had if you were in the same situation. What was this guy doing? Why was he looking at them? Then, to make matters worse, the guy suddenly got up from his seat, walked up the aisle, and sat down right in front of them. He slowly turned around in his seat and again stared right at them.

By this point, Louie's awkwardness was surpassed only by his indignation, so he finally said, "What's your problem?" The guy just smiled back at him and launched into a long story about how the movie was shot in his town and he was chosen as an extra. He was in a particular scene and couldn't wait to see himself in it. This is understandable; any of us would probably be as excited as he was.

Then he told Louie and his wife that this would be the sixth time he had seen the movie in the theater. But he seemed to be as excited as if it were the first time. He didn't say anything about staring at Louie and his wife, and Louie didn't ask. This guy must have just been so eager to talk to someone about his role that he locked on to them until they spoke to him.

Mercifully, the lights soon dimmed and the movie began. The story went along as usual, and Louie soon began to notice some of the parts of the story this guy had described. Sure enough, the guy's scene came up, and in a flash, he was on and off the screen. He turned around in his seat once more and flashed a huge, ear-eating grin.

Louie gave him a big thumbs-up.

I want to be like the guy in that theater. I want to be so excited to be an extra in God's story that I will tell anyone about it at any time (without the staring, of course). I want to beam with joy at the small part I play, never tiring of seeing how the story will play out and not harboring secret ambitions for a bigger part.

Being this type of extra requires that I drown my visions of personal glory in a sea of humility. I need to recognize that my place is not to write my own part in God's story. The mind-set of an extra, to go where the director says to go and do what the director says to do, will help me weaken my tendency to judge others. After all, the playing field is level for all the extras, so one extra has no reason to feel more important than the rest.

I am prone to extremes, so when I realized I am far better off cultivating the mind-set of an extra rather than a star, I became enamored with the thought of being completely unnoticed altogether. I wondered if my cravings for more of God were misguided. Maybe God wanted me to live out a simple life with no ambition for accomplishing great things for His kingdom.

But God is always faithful to bring me back from the zealousness of one mountaintop or another to the wisdom of the valley, and He occasionally sends me into a situation that broadens my perspective, reminding me that He is directing this story and will make use of me as He sees fit.

One such reminder came one evening as I had dinner with a large group of coworkers at a restaurant in Chicago. The guy sitting across from me was Jewish, and we somehow began talking about kosher foods. Others soon joined in the conversation, and I heard my internal pager begin to beep. Wanting to be like Dr. Mindy, I decided to answer it, so I turned the discussion to matters of religion.

Soon after, one of the guys to my left asked what religion I was, and I told him I was a Christian. "Yeah, but what kind of Christian?" he responded. I get this question all the time—a sad commentary that Christians are so divided, we have to explain what particular version of Jesus we follow. Not wanting to engage in a doctrinal debate, I told him simply: "I believe in the God of the Bible, and I love Jesus." He laughed; I'm not sure anyone had ever said "I love Jesus" to him.

The conversation went on. We dialogued about the existence of God and absolute truth, and we discussed Jesus' deity, ministry, crucifixion, and resurrection. We talked about sin, our need for repentance, the forgiveness that comes by faith, and even heaven and hell. When it was all said and done, I had been able to lay out the gospel for these guys to hear.

No doubt you've felt the joy that comes from sharing the gospel with someone, particularly if it was something you were nervous talking about in the first place. That was an important part of the story, but it wasn't what I took away from that night.

During the conversation, I remember thinking about more than the topics at hand or even the guys involved in the discussion. In fact, I thought a lot about myself. I thought about how great it was that God was using me to do work for His kingdom. I noticed how smart I was to answer all of their questions in the right way and how courageous I was to say things like "I love Jesus" to these guys.

Essentially, I was all too aware of what I was doing and not all that aware of what God was doing through me.

What kind of guy thinks about how great he is while he's sharing about how great God is? I guess I'm that type of guy, so I'm a perfect example of an extra believing the story is all about him. I might as well have entered Jesus' dressing room and plopped down in His chair, completely unaware that He was already sitting there. This kind of thinking did not fit with my new approach to being an extra and living a life that was commonplace in God's kingdom.

But this wasn't the end of the story. Soon after dinner had concluded, another coworker named Jim came up to me and said he had been listening in on our conversation. He shared that he had recently started attending a church and had just finished reading Matthew and Mark for the first time. The things he heard in our conversation validated what he had heard at church and solidified what he had been reading in the Gospels. I could see in his eyes that God had used this conversation to confirm something in his heart. He had clearly experienced a God-moment.

I didn't even know Jim was listening. He hadn't said a word the entire time, and I hadn't paid any attention to him. My version of the story was that I was sharing the gospel with these three other guys, and that was it. I didn't even know that the Director had another plot twist in mind. He knew the story He was telling, and He knew when and where each person should enter the stage.

So I felt bad about thinking of myself so much, and I told God I was sorry I had made myself the star of the night, but it only made the question of how to serve God more confusing. I know that sharing my faith is a good thing, but if it just leads to me thinking about how great I am, is it worth it? Am I better off serving God irrespective of what it does to me, or is it better to pull all the logs out of my own eye before attending to the specks in others'? How can I do good deeds that honor God instead of honoring me, all the while still pursuing the perspective of an extra?

If you've ever found yourself asking similar questions, take heart. Jesus gives us a few clues in the Sermon on the Mount:

> Don't do your good deeds publicly, to be admired, because then you will lose the reward from your Father in heaven…Give your

gifts in private…When you pray, don't be like the hypocrites who love to pray publicly…where everyone can see them…Go away by yourself, shut the door behind you, and pray to your Father secretly…When you fast, don't make it obvious…so people will admire [you] for [your] fasting…Comb your hair and wash your face. Then no one will notice that you are fasting, except your Father, who knows what you do in private.[5]

This sounds quite clear: Do everything in secret before the Father, which means not doing anything for others to see. But one chapter earlier, Jesus seemed to say something different to the same crowd:

You are the light of the world…No one lights a lamp and then puts it under a basket. Instead, a lamp is placed on a stand, where it gives light to everyone in the house. In the same way, let your good deeds shine out for all to see, so that everyone will praise your heavenly Father.[6]

So why does Jesus tell us, "Let your good deeds shine out for all to see," but also, "Don't do your good deeds publicly, to be admired"?

This reminds me of my tendency to elevate my own importance in God's work, to think of myself as one of the stars instead of an extra. I think Jesus is telling me (and you too if you think life is all about you) to keep in mind *why* we do what we do. He is calling our motives into question. God doesn't simply find satisfaction in our ability to do good deeds themselves; He also cares about our reason for doing them. He wants us to do them for Him so He may be glorified both in our hearts and in our hands.

This must be why Jesus says we should not do our good deeds publicly, *to be admired.* The minute our philanthropy and charity and service become about us—about our need to feel at peace with others by the good we do for society, or about our need to fill a lack of purpose with the admiration of others—we depart from the purity of the deed itself. In doing so, we minimize the glory God receives from our actions.

God is glorified when the lights of His children shine brightly for all to see, because others will see them and give Him praise. He is also glorified when His children give and pray and fast in secret, because they demonstrate that He is more desirable than the admiration of men.[7] So as long as we do our deeds in order to bring God glory, whether in secret or in public, they serve to make much of God instead of making much of ourselves.

For someone who has made a life out of making much of myself, passing judgments on others in order to make me feel better, and dreaming of the part of a lead character, Jesus' words take the strength from my legs and the pride from my heart. When I look down on others, Jesus tells me to love them as myself. When I embrace the role of star, Jesus tells me to become an extra. C.S. Lewis creates a compelling case for this kind of humility in *Mere Christianity:*

> Whenever we find that our religious life is making us feel that we are good—above all, that we are better than someone else—I think we may be sure that we are being acted upon, not by God, but by the devil. The real test of being in the presence of God is, that you either forget about yourself altogether or see yourself as a small, dirty object. It is better to forget about yourself altogether.[8]

The life of an extra, then, is to not think too highly of oneself. In fact, as Lewis notes, it is better not to think of ourselves at all. But forgetting about ourselves does not mean we, as the millions of extras called to the stage at this moment and at this time, are to forget to play the parts we have been given to play in God's story, whether those parts are big or small ones. Some of us will be asked to play small roles for most of our lives, and others may be asked to play bigger ones. But every one of us, as extras worthy of Jesus, will want to see His story played out for His sake and to His praise.

This picture of millions of extras all filling in the story of redemptive history is echoed in another metaphor: Paul's analogy of the church as the body of Christ. He writes, "Just as each of us has one body with many members, and these members do not all have the same function, so in Christ we who are many form one body, and each member belongs to all the others. We have different gifts, according to the grace given us."[9]

In comparing the church to our bodies, Paul seems to be saying something important about us. He implies each and every member is necessary and valuable to the success of the whole.

If you have ever broken a toe or jammed a finger or gotten something in your eye, you know how closely connected all the body's parts are to one another. All movement ceases, and your world centers on that very point of pain. At times, we may even stop whatever we're doing entirely until we fix whatever is causing the problem. And if the problem is a persistent one, such as a broken toe, the body limps along until the toe is fully restored.

The comparison to the body of Christ should be evident. When one part of the body is out of place or is hurting, the rest of the body suffers as well. The body is not able to accomplish the fullness of its purpose unless all its members are working together in unison. Our marriages and our churches and our communities all need this kind of unity if the body of Christ is to fulfill its mission of declaring God's glory and making disciples of all the nations.[10]

No doubt you have heard the analogy of the body of Christ, but the critical point I have learned is this: Being a little toe requires a great deal of humility.

If God means for me to be a little toe in the body of Christ, the body would not benefit at all if I tried to be an ear. I would complain about being a little toe, and I would make a mockery of my toeness when I hopped around trying to hear everything.

But the real tragedy would be that I would not be doing the job of a little toe. After all, if I were not there to do the little toe's job, the job wouldn't get done, or it would have to be done by a finger or an eyelash at the cost of their job as well. To cause the body of Christ to suffer on account of my own pride would be a shameful thing.

So embracing my toeness means wanting to make much more of God than myself. Wanting so much more of God in this way also means desiring to see Jesus receive all the adulation He deserves as the star. It means dressing in Jesus' kind of humility and forgetting ourselves as we are absorbed into the beauty and grandness of the story. This kind of humility, the kind that aligns every member of the body joyfully in its place, binds the body of Christ in unity so that it grows larger and stronger each day.

If we dress in this kind of humility as we go about our lives, being toes and ears and hands and teeth in the body of Christ, we will find a growing sense of love for the other members of the body. We might even stop making judgments about others, realizing that they are all extras like we are and that the point of the story isn't about us anyway. We might find ourselves grinning at people everywhere we go because we cannot wait to tell them all about this amazing story in which we find ourselves.

And as we grin and tell people about our part in this grand story, God looks back at us, smiles, and gives us a big thumbs-up.

8. Different:

God Is Different

People who are cold often like a hot drink.

Or so I'm told. I don't drink coffee, and I don't like milk, so I don't drink hot chocolate very often either. I only occasionally drink hot tea. But ski resorts and cities like Seattle and Portland and New York seem to be filled with shops that serve hot drinks. Drinks that are warmer than the outside air must make cold people feel better. That makes perfect sense.

All of this profundity filtered through my mind as I drove down Sanders Road in a suburb north of Chicago. I had just driven away from a client's office on a brutally cold night and was heading off to my hotel to spend a quiet evening doing something other than work. Leaving the company's complex, I had waited at the exit in my rental car while a bundled-up policeman, sporting a handheld beacon, directed traffic.

No doubt you have seen powerful searchlights that create burning columns of curiosity in the sky. They often surround stadiums during big sporting events or casinos that need just a few more people's savings. They're like the light to signal Batman but without the bat. Well, this policeman had a mini-version of one of those lights, but in red. He stuck it right in my eyes until it was safe to pull out of the complex. He didn't seem to mind that after his "signal" to go, I couldn't see anything but an enormous burned-out circle everywhere I looked. But I hit the gas anyway and turned left onto the street.

As I accelerated down the road, slowly regaining sight in the huge burned-out circle in front of my car, I saw another policeman about a quarter of a mile in front of me. He too was standing in the median strip while directing traffic, but he was at a smaller gate and therefore did not have as much to do. At this point, my car's heater hadn't warmed up much, so I was still pretty cold, and the thought occurred to me that this guy must be unbearably cold. That is when the revelation poured over me: People who are cold often like a hot drink.

After passing this second policeman, I made a U-turn at the next turn lane and headed back down the same street I had just driven, intending to slow down briefly beside him, stick my head out my window, and say, "Good evening. It looks pretty cold out here. Would you like me to get you a cup of coffee or hot chocolate?" I thought this would be just what he needed. Never mind that he would be taking coffee from a stranger; I figured that when a man is really, really, ridiculously cold, as this man must have been, he will take a hot drink from a grizzly bear.

I thought of Christ, standing as King before all the nations of the world in judgment, separating the sheep on His right and the goats on His left, saying to those on His right, "I was thirsty, and you gave me drink...when you did it to one of the least of these my brothers and sisters, you were doing it to me!"[1] If I am to understand this passage correctly, it appears when I give a thirsty man a drink, I give a thirsty Jesus a drink. I don't know if this man was thirsty, but I am quite certain he was cold, and I thought the principle still applied.

As I drove toward the policeman, I noted my surroundings in order to ensure my offer to him was made in safety. No cars were in front of me as far as I could see, and no cars were behind me either. So the road was essentially empty except for me and this policeman. As I slowed, I simultaneously rolled down my window and started to say, "Good eve—" But before I could finish my invitation, I heard a piercing yell out of the darkness.

"DON'T STOP ON THE ROAD! WHAT ARE YOU THINKING?"

Not wanting to disobey a cop, I quickly accelerated past him, hearing, "What kind of idiot stops on a road?" as I rolled up the window.

Hmm.

That is what I thought to myself for a good five seconds. I realized *I* must be the kind of idiot who stops on a road. I admit I was a little taken aback, and I experienced a momentary lapse into self-righteousness: *Well, fine! If you're going to be like that, you can freeze to death for all I care.* But my indignation slowly thawed as I continued to drive.

So I initiated another U-turn and headed back toward my new, cold, grumpy friend. Because he had strongly discouraged me from stopping on the road on my previous attempt, I thought of a new approach. Directly across the road from this man was an entrance to another office complex. I decided to park there, put on my hazard lights, and brave the cold to make my offer face-to-face.

As soon as I got out of the car, the policeman started waving his arms around. I thought, *Surely he must be waving me toward him.* So I looked both ways for traffic and, seeing none for at least half a mile, began walking across the street. I heard another piercing yell out of the darkness.

"DO *NOT* CROSS THE STREET! IT'S NOT SAFE OUT HERE! GO BACK TO YOUR CAR!"

I could not see what was so dangerous about two men talking on an empty road at night. But he was a cop, so he must have known more about this sort of thing than me. At that point, I deduced he was, in fact, waving me *away* from him, not toward him. So I dutifully returned to the side of my automobile, now intent on yelling my offer across the street. I thought he might respond better to communication of his kind.

The only problem was that a stream of traffic appeared on the road at that moment, and I could not say anything that could be heard for at least 30 seconds as the cars passed by. So I waited by my car in the cold, and he continued to wave his arms around and yell unintelligible things in my direction.

You might have left at this point, and you would have been smart to do so, but I did not. After all the cars had passed, and we were again alone on the road, I finally yelled across the street, "HI! I'M SORRY FOR THE CONFUSION. I JUST WANTED TO KNOW IF YOU WANTED—"

He apparently knew what I was going to say because he cut me off again.

"I CAN'T HEAR YOU! GET AWAY FROM HERE! IT'S DANGEROUS! GET AWAY! YOU'RE BEING WATCHED BY A SECURITY CAMERA. GET AWAY!"

Perhaps he didn't know what I was going to say after all. Clearly, he didn't care. After a while, I concluded that our dialogue wasn't going to happen as planned. I thought of a number of other ways I could bring this guy coffee, but I finally gave up and drove off, content to quit trying to show him Christ's love and instead just to think about it, which is always the easier thing to do, right?

So what happened that night? One thing is for sure: The man stayed cold. And he deserved it, I say.

Wait—I'm just kidding. I think. I know the reason I first thought about stopping was this notion that Jesus was thirsty or cold or hungry and that I could do something about it, which seems to be a good enough reason by itself. But I'm finding that something deeper is always going on when God is involved.

I assume Jesus was teaching me something about His kind of love. When I say I love others, He expects me to love them the same way I love Him. And I say I would do anything for Jesus, even give my life for Him. So does that mean I would give my life for this cop? This same man, the one I thought could freeze to death just because he wasn't kind to me? I'm not sure I would.

But in spite of my own fickle heart, I was still there, doing something I wouldn't normally do, thinking about someone else instead of living in my own little world the way I do most days. And I didn't see any other drivers stopping to talk to these cops either. So something out of the ordinary was going on that night, and this reminded me of some of the silliness you've already observed in my life.

Let's go back to something awkward: How about trying to stick a note in some young girl's bag? Or we could go with something embarrassing instead: How about sitting on a folding chair in front of a sign that says, "Ask anything about God" in front of a thousand snickering people? Or perhaps delusional is more your cup of coffee: How about believing I could master the practice of prayer, something history's greatest saints have wrestled with all of their lives, with three weeks and a little green sticky note?

These things seem awkward, embarrassing, and delusional, but they are also somewhat convicting, inspiring, and encouraging. Let's be honest; all of them make me (and you, whenever you do things like them) a little weird. But I'm also seeing something important in my pursuit of Christ, in my desperate attempt to shed the cloak of comfortable Christianity, in my cravings for more of God.

I've now realized God is different, and I suppose I've always suspected this to some degree, which is why I have tried all these things that were weird and different. This concept—God is different—is almost not even worth saying. When I take the time to think about it, it is, of course, quite obvious. God is God, and we are not, so He must be different. He even spells this out for us in Scripture, where He says, "My ways are higher than your ways and my thoughts higher than your thoughts."[2] He is the light to our darkness, the big to our small, the hot to our cold.

In order to get a better understanding of this concept, let's play a little game called If I Were God. The point of the game is to figure out what we would have done were we in God's position and then see how close we can come to the real God's decisions. We'll start with the account of King Hezekiah.[3]

Hezekiah was one of the good kings in the Old Testament. He ascended to the throne of the southern kingdom of Judah at the age of 25, and he cleansed the temple, tore down all the altars built to foreign gods, and restored worship to a nation who had forsaken their God. "He trusted in the Lord…so that there was none like him among all the kings of Judah after him, nor among those who were before him…And the Lord was with him; wherever he went out, he prospered."[4]

Fourteen years into his reign, Jerusalem was besieged by the Assyrians, but God struck down Judah's enemies, killing 185,000 in one night. The sight of God's mighty hand, if not the stench of death, must have left a lifelong impression on Hezekiah. So he continued leading his people, and God blessed him so that he was held in great esteem by all the surrounding nations. When he fell deathly sick, God heard his prayer and healed him, even adding 15 years to his life.

But eventually, late in his life, Hezekiah became comfortable and proud, forgetting what his God had done for him. In an act of royal pride, he paraded a Babylonian envoy around his entire kingdom. As a consequence, the prophet Isaiah came to him to tell him God would bring destruction on his house and that sons of his line would be carried off to Babylon and made into eunuchs. How did Hezekiah respond to this terrible news? "'The word of the LORD that you have spoken is good.' For he thought, 'Why not, if there will be peace and security in my days?'"[5]

IF I WERE GOD, I would have gone ballistic. I would have struck him with boils or sent Babylon back to lead him off in chains, making a eunuch out of him in front of all his people. Sure, this guy had been a great king and had done all sorts of righteous things, but after I delivered him miraculously from the hand of his enemy, spared his life when he was on his deathbed, *and* gave him 15 more years of life, he starts showing off and looking out for number one?

But God is not like me at all; in fact, He waited a hundred years to carry out His judgment, and Hezekiah ultimately died in peace. So I didn't do so well on this round. Let's try another.

Scripture says that God considered King David, Israel's second and most revered king, to be "a man after his own heart."[6] As you may know, David was chosen by God to be king even while he was a young shepherd. David made a name for himself, becoming a great warrior, and after running from King Saul for years, he was finally installed as the people's king. He defeated all of Israel's enemies, brought the ark of the covenant back to Jerusalem, and pleased the Lord so much that God made a covenant with him to establish His eternal kingdom through David's line (a prophecy about the Messiah).

All was well with David until one year when he did not go out with his men to battle. Staying behind, he loitered in his palace, and he happened to see a beautiful woman bathing. He sent for her, slept with her, impregnated her, and had her husband murdered, finally taking her as his wife. When the prophet Nathan came to him and told him an allegory of his own sin, David even cast judgment on himself unawares. Only when he was confronted with what he had done did he come clean, finally repenting to the Lord.

IF I WERE GOD, I don't know what I would have done to David, but I would have done something. Perhaps I would have struck him with a sickness, or maybe I would have sent enemies to attack him. Maybe if I had been in a really good mood, I would have had mercy on him altogether, hearing his cries of repentance and forgiving him for what he had done. After all, he was (or at least had been) the man after my own heart, right?

But God did something quite different: He spared David's life, and He instead took the life of this love child on the seventh day after his birth.[7] What? Wait a minute! This innocent baby didn't do anything. Why did he bear the punishment his father deserved? This wasn't fair—what was God doing? Isn't He a just and loving God?

Or how about the time King David brought the ark of the covenant, Israel's most prized possession, to Jerusalem, the seat of the nation and the future site of God's temple? You may remember what happened. David and all Israel went up to Kiriath-jearim, where the ark was located, loaded it on a cart, and headed for home. The two drivers of the cart, Uzzah and Ahio, must have felt like this was a pretty important responsibility. This was the ark of their living God! They went along their merry way until all of a sudden, the oxen stumbled, and the ark began to slip. So Uzzah put out his hand to steady the ark and keep it from falling. Seems like a great thing, right?

IF I WERE GOD, I would reward this man for his quick mind and quicker hands, perhaps moving in David's heart to promote Uzzah or stand him before the people of Israel and tell them all how he had saved God's ark from crashing to the ground. But God did something else entirely. His anger burned against Uzzah, and He killed him that day because of Uzzah's presumptuous error in touching the ark.

I'm finding that this game isn't working out too well. If God is a good God, I would apparently be a terrible God. To be completely honest, though, my answers reveal that I actually think I would make a better God than God. After all, my responses seem like they would be fair in my own mind, and I don't know that I can say the same about God's. Perhaps you share my sentiments.

If you remember, we started with the realization that God is different from us, and we're seeing just how different He really is. He's way different, far beyond anything I'm really comfortable believing if I were to be totally honest. He does things that violate my sense of justice and desecrate my understanding of love. We can talk all day about craving God, but some of these accounts from the Bible beg the question, am I sure I want so much more of this God?

After all, this is the God who made a perfect man and put him in a garden with two trees, one that would bring life and one that would bring death.[8] Wouldn't the garden have been better with just the one tree?

This is the God who created the heavens and the earth and man and called them good (He even called man "very good") and then a short time later decided He was sorry He had made them, ultimately deciding to flood the entire earth.[9] If God knew this would happen, why not just make better people in the first place?

This is the God who hardened Pharaoh's heart, who raised up this leader in order to demonstrate His power, bringing plague after plague and ultimately death to him and his people.[10] How was this fair to Pharaoh?

This is the God who planned and predestined the beatings, torture, and murder of His beloved Son.[11] Couldn't God's plan have been accomplished without the gut-wrenching agony and blood-spurting sport of Roman execution?

We shudder at the prospect of a God so terrifying and powerful, but this is also the God who loved the world so much that He sent His one and only Son to suffer and die that horrible death because of what it means for us.[12] Who are we that we merit this kind of sacrifice?

This is also the God who turned the fiercest enemy of the early church into its greatest missionary.[13] Who was Paul that he was counted worthy of this mercy and honor?

This is also the God who "chose us in him before the foundation of the world," saving us by His grace through our faith irrespective of anything we have ever done.[14] Who are we to receive the glorious inheritance of Christ without doing anything to deserve it?

This is also the God who has gone to prepare a place for His followers, who is coming back again to do away with sin and death and tears, who will create a new heaven and a new earth, and who will dwell with His people forever.[15] Who are we, such fragile and insignificant beings, that we should enjoy all of eternity with this amazing God?

This is also the God who takes it personally when we offer food to the hungry, drink to the thirsty, hospitality to the stranger, clothes to the naked, companionship to the imprisoned, comfort to the sick, and perhaps even coffee to the cold. What kind of marvelous God is this who identifies with the weakest of humanity?

God *is* different. He's much more terrifying than I had imagined but also so much more glorious and beautiful than I thought possible. I've spent too many years glossing over hard truths about God in favor of pleasant ones in an attempt to make Him more palatable to my taste or softer to the touch of others' ears. In the process, I have developed inch-deep beliefs about a mile-high God.

I know this is hard to deal with intellectually, emotionally, and spiritually, but the simplicity and cogency of Scripture bring us face-to-face with a God who takes our sin and His holiness really seriously. He takes love and mercy seriously too. If A.W. Tozer was correct when he said that "what comes into our minds when we think about God is the most important thing about us," then we have no choice but to embrace the smooth wine and the hardtack of God's descriptions of Himself.[16] When we are tempted not to savor the wine or to spit out the hardtack, we must resist the urge to adjust our beliefs about God to suit our sensibilities.

It seems that when we encounter a hard truth about God, we either bend our understanding to Him or bend Him to our understanding.

For those of us who find we are guilty of bending God to our understanding, we would do well to take note of the well-worn, battle-tested, God-centered theology that John Piper intimates when he says, "When God is seen with edges (He is this, and He's not that), I can know Him. This is Him; that's not Him. This is worth dying for; that's not worth dying for. Clear, precise [knowledge] about God, about Christ, about faith, about the cross, about the Holy Spirit awakens [our] passions."[17]

We could think of Dr. Piper's words in another way: We see true things about God in the full revelation of Scripture, and we begin to believe untrue things about God when we ignore some parts of His revelation in favor of others. The true things are worth dying for, and they're worth living for. The untrue things are not.

I now understand I have spent too many years trying to polish God's edges or ignore them altogether because believing in Him is easier when He doesn't challenge my beliefs about Him than when He does. After all, if I believe in a God who does things I would never do, what does that say about me?

But I'm learning to see the goodness in God's edges. When Dr. Piper says clear, precise knowledge about God awakens our passions, I believe him because I recognize the glory and grandeur of worshipping a God whose ways and thoughts are higher than my own. And when I ask myself if I really want so much more of this God, the answer is yes, but my answer has more gravity than it did before because I now feel I have to mean it from somewhere deeper within my soul. Maybe this is because believing hard things about God costs more than believing easy things.

I'm learning that just because something is hard, that doesn't mean it's not true. Comfortable Christians do easy things while Christ-followers do hard things.[18] Picking up our crosses daily is hard, loving our enemies is hard, turning the other cheek is hard, and embracing the holiness of God that envelopes the hardtack of His wrath and the sweet wine of His mercy is hard. The hard things require serious answers to our questions about this God we crave.

Thinking about these kinds of Christ-honoring, edge-affirming, hard things takes me back to the awkward, embarrassing, and delusional actions we talked about earlier, like sticking a note in some young girl's bag or sitting on a folding chair in the middle of a mall and asking people to give me their theological best shot. If you were to ask me what hard things I've done for God, I would probably point to those. And they were hard, and they were different, but they weren't the hardest kinds of things.

I suppose the hardest kinds of things are rarely external; they are almost always the exploration of what's inside us. I can face the fears of street witnessing with just a little courage and companionship from other Christian weirdoes, but it's far more terrifying to excavate the reasons why I spend most of the time in that chair making judgments of the people I meet. And even that doesn't sound so bad when compared to digging deeper and finding a belief that God may not save the people I'm talking to because He chose not to save them before they were even born.

We all must eventually answer this question: What happens when we look deep inside? What if we find something about ourselves we don't want to discover? Even worse, what if we find out something about God we don't want to know?

These are tough questions with no easy answers, but my cravings for more of God tell me to keep digging. I'm finding that a soul saturated in Scripture will ultimately find the pure water of God's supreme difference deep beneath the surface, and this different kind of water, a living kind of water, satisfies.[19]

I don't know if these questions and thoughts scare you or bore you, but I invite you all the same to consider how different this living water, the kind of water that never makes you thirsty again, truly is. Our consideration should bring to mind all sorts of questions, and they're not the easy kind of questions we would probably prefer.

How badly do we want this kind of water? Are we willing to ask Jesus for it? Are we willing to do hard things like being weirdoes for Christ when He tells us to do things we'd rather not? Are we open to doing harder things like examining the parts of our hearts we've hidden for so long? Are we ready to do the hardest things like embracing the God of the Bible in all His glorious fury and tenderness?

I raise a toast to those of you who have decided to drink this different kind of water, believing all the while that it will not only satisfy our cravings for God but also change us in the process. As He goes about changing us, we will begin to more easily turn the other cheek when hit, show love in response to hate, and even show kindness to heat-starved, grumpy cops. He will grant us the courage to examine our own hearts against the purity of His Son. And He will give us the wisdom to rethink everything we believe about Him, using the sweeping wind of Scripture to blow away the chaff of our superficial faith.

After all, God is in the process of making us different, just like Him.[20]

9. Rules:

How God Changes
All of the Rules

I thought about inventing a new kind of ruler, but it didn't work out.

It was a bandwagon type of idea, trying to capitalize on the trend a lot of companies are following in tailoring their products to individual tastes. For example, you can get a credit card with the logo of your choice, a car that shoots flames out the exhaust, or a birthday cake with your face on it. Toothbrushes now sport hundreds of options. Mobile phones are no longer functional items—they are accessories, and you can get your accessory in almost any shape or color you want.

I thought I could get in on this game and make a few bucks in the process. So I reviewed many of the commonplace products that appear in nearly every home, thinking perhaps some of them could be updated to reflect more personal times. I sketched out plans for brooms with downloadable ring tones, garbage bags with the family photo imprinted on them, and even monogrammed meats, but none of those concepts went anywhere. Then one day, I came across the perfect item, something that hangs on every workbench wall, sits in every kitchen junk drawer, or lies beneath every rolltop desk: the ruler.

I would call my new kind of ruler "The FreeRuler—the Ruler with No Rules!" It would be brilliant.

The premise was simple: Customers could construct their own ruler any way they see fit. Just think of the possibilities! No longer would mankind be constrained by society's systems of measurement. Gone would be the days in which we are forced to report measurements with standard terminology. The ruler would escape the dark ages of traditionalism and join the rest of progressive society. Every forward-thinking person would want one.

However, the FreeRuler would not stop at custom colors, personalized initials, or even a long and narrow picture of your choice on the underside. Instead, the FreeRuler would take customization to the next level so that each and every person could truly make the ruler their own. Customers could select the ruler's units of measure—they could use existing ones, like inches or millimeters, or they could create their own units, like spalsties or wonkies. The distance between units would be specified according to individual tastes. Rulers would become like snowflakes, with no two alike.

Things were going great with this idea until I shared my plan with some potential investors. They weren't too excited about it—something about wanting to make a profit. People these days are evidently so stuck in the comfort of the past that they never want to take a risk on a bold vision like the FreeRuler.

I was disappointed, but at the end of the day, I found myself with a product with no market. And I wondered why the FreeRuler would not sell. Why do people want some products customized to every extent possible, but they prefer the normal, boring, same-as-it's-always-been qualities in other items?

Someone smart like you immediately knows why the FreeRuler would never work: Rulers with no standards are useless. And if you are at all philosophical, you may already be making the connection between the ruler and morality.

The ruler is useful to us because it has actual standards. Let's say you are trying to pick out a new sofa at a furniture store, and you call me and ask me to run over to your place and measure how much space is in your living room. I go and measure with my prototype FreeRuler and tell you it's 18 wonkies. That won't do you any good, will it?

The same idea holds true when we talk about some kind of moral ruler or standard that tells us whether we're good or bad people. Nearly all of us think of ourselves as good people, but unless we have an actual standard to measure against, good and bad really don't mean anything.

This is why relativism, or the philosophy that says there's no real standard, is so absurd. A man can make up his own version of truth, and I can make up my own wonky-based system of measurement, but neither will be of any use to anyone. I suppose the FreeRuler could be the measuring instrument of choice for the relativist, so perhaps I could find a growing market after all.

We seem to know standards are good things, judging from the way we react to situations that come up in our lives. Suppose you are a student who studies hard and does well in school. Imagine then that every college you wanted to attend accepted students based on birth month rather than grades. Wouldn't you cry foul? Or suppose you are a hardworking employee, and all the promotions at your job were determined by shoe size rather than work performance. Wouldn't you scream, "No fair!"

So if we are going to have opinions about what is right or fair, we don't seem to have much choice but to acknowledge a standard beyond ourselves to appeal to in the first place. C.S. Lewis writes eloquently about this whole business of truth and right and wrong and standards, which he calls the Law of Human Nature. In his discussion, he makes this point:

> Whenever you find a man who says he does not believe in a real Right and Wrong, you will find the same man going back on this a moment later. He may break a promise to you, but if you try breaking one to him he will be complaining "It's not fair" before you can say Jack Robinson...it seems, then, we are forced to believe in a real Right and Wrong. People may be mistaken about them, just as people sometimes get their sums wrong; but they are not a matter of mere taste and opinion any more than the multiplication table.[1]

If Lewis is an accurate observer of human nature, then he's confirming what we learned from the FreeRuler: An actual standard must exist. We all live in light of this standard whether we acknowledge it or not. We have an internal bar to measure ourselves against, something to compare ourselves to, and we build all sorts of rules in our lives based on what we believe this standard to be. If we believe the Bible is the standard, we hunt through its pages for rules to follow, looking to do those things that will help us measure up and feel like good Christians. If we believe society is the standard, we do our best to not break any of the society's rules so we can be good citizens.

I'm guilty of this. I often use other people as the standard I measure myself against. As long as I'm doing better than that guy, I feel pretty good about myself. Of course, this only works if that guy is someone other than Jesus, the one who set and met the standard.

I imagine I'm not the only comfortable Christian, or any kind of person for that matter, who is intent on following a set of rules. Many of us crave more of God, and we often think we will satisfy that craving as we do more

"Christian" things. Or we think that being a solid Christian means being a better rule follower than most of the Christians we know.

I suppose our families often contribute to these feelings. For many of us, Mom and Dad set certain boundaries when we were kids, and they rewarded us for following the rules and punished us for breaking them, so we turn out to be self-interested rule-followers who spend our lives working out our guilt. Or maybe some of us had no rules at all and turned out to be rotten people, and we operate under the delusion that freedom from rules means freedom from guilt. It doesn't take too many toys or spankings before the idea of conditional acceptance begins to creep into our psyches.

Our churches sometimes don't do us any favors in this regard. Many denominations offer their own set of unwritten (or written) rules to follow: no smoking, no drinking, no dancing, no movies, no caffeine, no bookstores in church, no raising of hands, no praying out loud, no confession of sin in small group, no laying on of hands to heal the sick, no speaking in tongues. And these rules don't only exist in the negative. In other churches, we have to wear a coat and tie or a long dress, support a certain church initiative, believe a certain set of creeds, speak in tongues, or give a certain amount of money to be counted among the faithful. Belonging to this kind of community means following its rules.

No wonder legalism begins to show up in the church. I don't mean to criticize our parents and teachers and pastors, because most of them do a wonderful job raising us and teaching us how to follow God. But if these authority figures accept us or reject us because of what we do or don't do, even in subtle ways, we will naturally believe God, our ultimate authority, accepts us or rejects us in the same way. This makes perfect sense. The people who love us the most seem to love us even more when we abide by whatever rules they consider to be good. And these people serve to shape so much of how we come to understand our heavenly Father.

I wondered if Christians struggle with this pressing weight of legalism more than other people do, but religious people of all kinds seem no better off than the best legalists Christianity has to offer.

Islam's Five Pillars and Sharia clearly mark the steps man is to take toward righteousness. Follow them closely lest you fail to attain heaven.

Buddhism's Four Noble Truths tell us to pursue the Noble Eightfold Path, which requires a man to think, speak, and do rightly in order to escape suffering, rebirth, and karma and to attain the detached state of parinirvana.

Hinduism's concept of karma (quite similar to Buddhism's) almost forces good behavior from its adherents—the certainty of cosmic retribution lingers over every act.

Jehovah's Witnesses talk about embracing Jesus as their Savior, but their conception of salvation is based on loyalty to the Watchtower Society and its members, which requires a great deal of work.

Mormons also talk about embracing Jesus as their Savior, but the Mormon conception of salvation requires God's grace in addition to man's obedience and faithfulness to certain practices and rituals of the Mormon Church.

And in the interest of fair play, we can even turn to the deist who embraces no institutional faith at all. Insisting he is beyond the crutch of man's religions, he still bows under legalism's weight, believing he can gain heaven only through a balance of life weighted toward being a good person. Even the man with no use for God is bound by his own arbitrary system of morality, developed in his own mind by what he feels is acceptable and unacceptable behavior. He will try his absolute best to hit his own target, even if it is a moving one.

So evidently, all kinds of people, religious and irreligious alike, believe that we should be good people and that we become good people by following some prescribed set of rules. If we don't follow these rules, we'll burn in hell, or we'll come back as a goat or a bug, or we'll go out of existence altogether. Something deep inside each one of us seeks to prove we are good enough—to our parents, our friends, ourselves, God. We do this because we know deep down that we aren't good enough, and the illusion of feeling like good people feels better than the reality of knowing we are not.

I have had many conversations with some really nice people about this sort of thing. I remember one lunch I had with a Jewish coworker who wasn't devout but identified strongly with his culture, and we talked for a long time about his interest in Jewish law and the year he spent in Israel after college. While he was there, he studied the Torah, part of which contained the law of Moses, which he understood to be a set of rules by which the Israelites should live.

We had an enjoyable conversation, and near the end of it, I remember asking him about God's laws and how he, as a Jew, felt about following them. He said, "I want to live a good life and have an impact on the world. I'm just not that comfortable with the thought of having to follow a certain set of rules in order to live a good life. I'm more interested in finding those rules I feel comfortable with and doing my best to follow those. And when it's over, I'm prepared to receive a just reward or punishment."

When my friend said he doesn't want to follow a certain set of rules, he seemed to me to be saying he doesn't want to follow the rules of the Torah. The fact that he's made his own set of rules shows how irresistible rules are, even to the nonreligious.

I could tell you about a number of similar conversations I've had that turned toward spiritual things and ended with something like this: "I believe a God is probably out there. And I'm a pretty good person; I haven't killed anyone, and I don't cheat on my wife. Sure, there are a few things I could do better; nobody's perfect, you know. But I think I'll go to heaven when I die because I haven't done anything really bad." I'm sure you've heard something like this too.

When I hear people make comments like these, I can't blame them too much because I have fallen into the same trap many times. I can play the part of a good reformed Protestant and yell *sola gratia* until I'm blue in the face, but I've spent many years living out my faith by following my own set of religious rules, such as "Read, pray, serve, and you'll be more spiritual," or "Don't drink, don't smoke, don't cuss, and don't borrow money...and oh, make sure no one else does any of those things either." I could go on, but the point is that legalism has found hospitality in my own home. Maybe it seeped through my windows over time, but it's been camped out on my couch for as long as I can remember.

I suppose if the whole point of life were to receive a just reward, or to keep from being punished, or even to go to heaven, and if God were fair in the way I would be IF I WERE GOD, then this way of thinking would make perfect sense. Religions make this their aim: Be good in order to be righteous.[2] In fact, if a philosophy or way of life offered something else entirely, affirming that true religion wasn't meant to be all about rules, well, that would be nothing short of different, wouldn't it?

Don't get me wrong. I'm not saying we should throw out all rules and proclaim either anarchistic freedom or universal salvation for everyone. God gave rules to man, starting in Eden, and He filled several pretty long books in the Old Testament with them. Jesus issued His fair share of commandments too. But I don't think the rules are the point. Instead, the rules point to the point, which is grace.[3]

You likely know what grace is all about, that it is favor from God that we don't deserve, so I won't belabor the point that grace is free, and that we can't earn grace, and that grace plus anything is no longer grace, and that salvation by faith through grace means that salvation is a gift from God irrespective of any good work we've ever done, and that the righteousness we have before God is credited to us because of Jesus' death on the cross on our behalf.[4]

All right, maybe I belabored it a little.

But my thought is that we're so conditioned to think of our relationship to God in terms of rules that grace becomes a religious word instead of a way of life. You may have even quickly skipped over the paragraph about grace because you've heard it all before. We don't think in terms of living by grace; it's something that happened to us once and something we sing about in church.

This is all fine and well, but it doesn't exactly help to just say, "Don't follow rules; embrace grace." That's like walking into rehab and telling a new patient: "Don't drink anymore; embrace sobriety!" It's just not that easy.

If we can't throw rules out altogether, then we should probably figure out what their purpose is. This is where God, who is different from all of man's religions, enters the stage. He didn't give rules to man simply to coerce right behavior. They didn't just provide a fair system by which He could make judgments about who was good enough. His rules existed for one purpose: To show all the people in the world that they don't measure up. Paul wrote about this to the Christians in Rome: "If it had not been for the law, I would not have known sin."[5]

You know this as well as I do: We don't need grace if we have no sin, and we don't have sin if we have no standard. So God—knowing how lovely grace would be, and that He would receive glory from showing this kind of grace, and that giving grace to humanity would serve to make much of Jesus rather than much of man—made rules He knew we would break. In fact, that was their very purpose!

So the law was God's way of showing us that we need Him. And needing God sounds a whole lot like a relationship, not like following rules.

I wanted to come up with an interesting way to illustrate that following rules simply cannot lead to a deepening relationship, so I asked Anna to write out a list of ten rules I could follow to deepen our love, thinking perhaps many of them would be along the same lines as our attempts to earn God's love through keeping His rules. In her first attempt, she came up with five items, like "Buy me more shoes" and "Give me a dog." That was a good list, and I'm going to hang on to it for future reference, but it wasn't quite what I was looking for. So I asked her to take one more shot at it and to focus on a more substantive list, one that would capture long-standing rules that would stand the test of time in a lifetime of marriage.

She came back to me half an hour later and said she couldn't do it; she said love wasn't about a list of things I could do for her. Sure, she just lost her chance at a dog, but the exercise made me think a bit more about the interplay between love and rules.

I wondered what our marriage would look like if it were completely based on rules. Suppose our wedding vows include some legalistic statements, such as "I promise not to sleep around," or "I'll give you a monthly allowance," or "I'll talk to you at least five minutes every night before bed." If I were to live my marriage by rising each day, pulling out my clipboard with Ten Things to Do in Order to Love Anna Today and making every effort to stick to the list, I suppose our marriage might not end in divorce, but it sure wouldn't go anywhere. We could ultimately fulfill the obligations of marriage without ever enjoying it.

But some of those rules, like "I promise not to sleep around," are actually good things. I don't want to sleep around, and if I ended up doing so, our relationship would be devastated. So that seems to be a good rule to follow, one that would keep us together. But again, if we were married for

30 years, and I didn't do anything other than not sleep around, something tells me that's not going to be good enough.

Perhaps rules don't create intimacy by themselves. Maybe they create the *space* for intimacy.

We can think of this another way: Following rules like these makes intimacy possible. In fact, staying within certain boundaries is the only way to deepen a relationship. A man cannot develop a soul-deep bond with his wife in an open marriage. But he also cannot develop a soul-deep bond with his wife by avoiding an open marriage and doing nothing else. Having a monogamous relationship simply creates the space for the man and his wife to develop trust, deepen their understanding of one another, and enjoy the intimacy that grows as two lives are joined into one.

The Bible compares the church's bond with Jesus to a marriage, so I think we can say similar things about our relationship with Him. We just saw how God's commandments served to highlight our sin so we'd know we needed God in the first place. We might like to leave the rules behind once we're justified, embracing grace, and moving beyond the old legalism of the past. But when we commit our lives to following Christ, the rules don't just suddenly disappear. In fact, Jesus stepped up the commands in many ways. So why did He do this?

I think Jesus' commandments create space for us to enjoy intimacy with Him. The night before His crucifixion, Jesus spent some quality time with His disciples in the upper room of a house in Jerusalem. You probably know this account well because this was when He washed their feet and instituted the Lord's Supper. While He was speaking to them, pouring into them all the words He longed to say before He left them, He made it very clear how His disciples should relate to His rules: "If you love me, you will keep my commandments."[6]

If we had been among the disciples, we might have been tempted to think back to the law, nodding our heads in agreement as if to say, "Ah, I see. So if we follow the law and obey all of Jesus' commandments, we'll be good to go, right?" Perhaps Jesus' statement would have been innocuous enough if that were all He said about it. But a few moments later, He said, "Whoever has my commandments and keeps them, he it is who loves me." And then, "If anyone loves me, he will keep my word…whoever does not love me does not keep my words." And finally, "If you keep my commandments, you will abide in my love."[7]

Let me try to summarize what Jesus said: If you love Jesus, you will keep His commandments, and whoever keeps His commandments loves Him, and if anyone loves Him, that person will keep His commandments, and if you keep His commandments, you will abide in His love. Does that help?

What was Jesus' point that night? Was He just repeating the same idea using slightly different words just so He could hear His own voice? No, He was making a point, a really important point: Love and obedience go together. Intimacy and rules go together. You can't separate one from the other.

This takes us back to obedience creating space for intimacy. We said that rules in a marriage make intimacy possible because they allow trust to develop and understanding to deepen as two lives are joined into one. Jesus made a similar point to His disciples using the picture of a vine and a branch. He said to them, "I am the vine; you are the branches. Whoever abides in me and I in him, he it is that bears much fruit, for apart from me you can do nothing."[8] When the branch obeys and abides in the vine ("if you keep my commandments, you will abide in my love"), space for intimacy is created as the vine and the branch become joined as one. In fact, no one can tell where the vine ends and the branch begins.

This takes us back to grace. None of this abiding or obeying or joining happens without grace. We said before that rules point to grace, and now we see how. Apart from the work of Jesus on the cross, our legalism acts as a blade that severs the branch from the vine. We end up dry and withered on the ground, waiting to be gathered and thrown into the fire. But through Jesus' death, through His grace, our obedience in faith allows our branch to abide in His vine, and His love begins to flow through us.

This takes us back to the ruler. Our desperate desire to measure up to some standard, whether we read it in Scripture or make it up on our FreeRuler, is doomed to failure. An isolated branch can't earn its way to the vine; it has to grow out from the vine. In the same way, we have to create space for intimacy through obedience in order to abide in Christ, to grow in our relationship with Him.

You may think me trendy to say, "It's not about religion, man. It's about a relationship." But I've spent so much energy over so many years trying to be a better Christian by praying harder and reading more often and serving more passionately, and those things haven't satisfied my cravings for more of God. They have only left me dry and withered.

If this doesn't resonate with you at all, you might be a few steps farther down the road of faith than me. But you might also be off the road altogether, mired in the rule-following pit so deep that it's above your eyes, and I'd encourage you to think back to the moment you first loved Jesus, because you probably didn't have any notions of rules then.

But if this strikes a chord in your heart, I invite you to continue on the journey with me. Let's give up, once and for all, this whole business of trying to measure up, to prove ourselves to God and to others by following a bunch of rules. And let's crave more of His grace, the grace that calls us to the cross of Jesus, where He eyes each one of us and asks, "Are you going to follow rules, or are you going to follow Me?"

10. Soldier:

How to Find Your Purpose in Combat Boots

How would you feel if you got shot for not obeying your boss?

I don't know about you, but I wouldn't like it one bit. I don't even like getting a bad review from my boss or not getting a raise I was expecting. If my boss were to actually shove me, I would probably report him to Human Resources. And if he were to hit me, I might even report him to the police. But if he shot me, I would be pretty upset, although I suppose I couldn't do much about it unless of course he just winged me.

Fortunately, I've never had to worry about this problem in my current job, which I consider to be one of its perks. I hope this isn't a day-to-day worry of yours either. But in one line of work in particular, obedience and loyalty to your boss could mean keeping your life or losing it: the military.

During my time in the Air Force, I actually disobeyed one of my commanders once. As a first lieutenant, I was put in charge of a program study to develop a really cool space rocket payload carrier thing that I can't really tell you much about. The situation was a little complicated because our headquarters, which was located at another base, put one of their officers on the program as well, and he was a major, which outranks a first lieutenant by two ranks. But because my boss (a general) outranked his boss (a colonel), I was put in charge of the study.

Awkward.

I was a young idealist at the time, full of testosterone and arrogance and distrustful of most kinds of authority, particularly those I didn't agree with. So when I decided our team needed to travel around the world, talking to the commanders who would actually be using this thing, and the major from headquarters told us not to do it, we decided to do it anyway.

So we went, hitting three continents and eight cities in seven days. Fortunately, I didn't get shot for this stunt and instead got a pretty sweet trip out of the deal, along with a little jet lag. The major wasn't real happy with me at first, but we ended up working things out. But other disobedient soldiers have not fared as well.

For thousands of years, military commanders have had to deal with disobedience in their ranks. Soldiers disobeyed their commanders in many ways, but perhaps the worst form was desertion, where soldiers simply ran away from their duties. If you were a commander, this was never a good scenario. You could track the guy down and kill him, track him down and imprison him, or just let him go altogether. In any case, you were short one soldier.

You might think just letting him go would be best. After all, if you're short one soldier no matter what, and if he deserted because his heart wasn't in the job, then you don't want him there anyway. But desertion has been considered "a disease, a cancer. [It] not only deplete[d] an army of soldiers but spread to those who remain[ed], undermining their morale and eroding unit cohesion."[1] This is why most commanders throughout the course of history have put their deserters to death. It violates our modern sensibilities, but the reason is clear enough: If my buddy and I are part of an army at war, and we both talk about running away, and he finally does it and is caught and shot, then I'm going to think twice about taking off when I'm tempted.

Ultimately, military commanders have a job to do. The best commanders inspire loyalty from their followers, but they are most concerned with absolute obedience. Complete obedience in battle means following orders, like "Don't shoot until I say so," and it often means the difference between life or death, victory or defeat. So it's in the best interest of commanders to exact obedience from their troops regardless of the cost.

As we know, God is altogether different from us. He is a commander in one sense, with armies of angels at His command and millions upon millions of committed followers, but He is unlike any commander on earth.

The army doesn't want your love, just your obedience. But God wants both.

Personally, I struggle with giving Him both. When I view God as my Commander and King, obeying Him seems easier than loving Him. Remember Uzzah, the cart driver who saved the ark from falling to the ground and was put to death by God for touching it? Or how about the story of Ananias and Sapphira, a couple in the early church who sold some property in order to give money to those in need? They lied about the amount, and God struck them dead as well.[2] Stories like these induce fear in my heart, and they remind me of times when I obeyed God solely because I was afraid of what He might do to me if I didn't.

However, when I view God as my Father and Friend, loving Him seems easier than obeying Him. When Jesus teaches us to pray to our Father, and when Paul calls us sons of God and brothers to Jesus, and when Jesus calls His disciples friends instead of servants, I'm not as fearful of God as I was before.[3] But before I know it, I'm walking around saying dumb things like "Jesus is my homeboy" without any proper respect for God.

We sense a tension in the ways the Spirit teaches us to view God or Jesus—Commander or Father, King or Friend, Master or Brother, Savior or Servant—and we probably shouldn't be that surprised by it. After all, we are a people who believe that one God exists in three persons, that Jesus was fully human and fully God, that the last will be first, and all sorts of other paradoxes that make no sense to some people.

As a guy who can focus on only one thing at a time, I struggle to sit with this tension because I would much prefer one or the other. I'd like to focus on loving God with all my heart, trying to go deep to find emotions and affections for Him. Or I could focus on obeying Him with all my heart, summoning my courage and will to do what He wants me to do.

This is why offering both love and obedience to God is difficult for me. But I know love and obedience are connected, because we just saw how Jesus tied the two together in a square knot of faith during the Last Supper with His disciples. You will recall His words: "If you love me, you will keep my commandments."[4] So how can this be possible?

One of the ways I've worked with this tension is by exploring the concept of purpose. I have spent years contemplating my life's purpose, and I'm sure you have thought about yours as well. We ask questions like "Why am I here?" and "What is my calling in life?" We talk to each other about the future, saying, "Yeah, man. I'm really trying to figure out my purpose right now—you know, what my calling is," as if we are constantly anxious to know exactly what God wants for us one day. Any of us who call ourselves committed Christ-followers would echo Isaiah's words, "Here am I! Send me," if only we knew what God was saying to us or asking us to do.[5]

Apart from that direction, we exhaust our spirits thinking about tomorrow, wondering when God is going to reveal our life's purpose to us, all the while ignoring Jesus' encouragement: "Do not be anxious about tomorrow, for tomorrow will be anxious for itself. Sufficient for the day is its own trouble."[6]

You might disagree with where I'm going with this, believing instead that being "created in Christ Jesus for good works, which God prepared beforehand, that we should walk in them" means we have to strive to figure out those good works ahead of time.[7] Perhaps this is even part of your own sense of craving for more of God—longing to know what He wants from you—because then you can go do it and feel good about doing it and ultimately satisfy that craving.

This strikes me as a bit self-centered and off target. It's self-centered because the focus turns from God's global, redemptive purposes to our local, individual purpose. This amounts to a soldier thinking his task is the same thing as the war. And it's off target because it replaces daily dependence on God through His Word and through prayer with autonomous destiny fulfillment. This is like a private going to the general and saying, "Just give me the orders, sir, and I'll be on my way. Don't burden me with a map or a radio."

But when I go back to Jesus' words and focus on today's troubles only, I still have a nagging sense of purpose, a feeling that life is fleeting, that I'm here for some reason, and that I'm going to waste my life if I don't figure out what that reason is. Figuring this out in hindsight is easy—I remember times when I felt God's hand move in my life, when I could see the purpose for something that happened to me, most particularly in times of pain or suffering. You probably know what I'm talking about. These are testimonies we share with people because they're just too powerful to be mere chance, and we know God was behind it all.

Of course, we rarely find that sense of purpose during the moment. I heard

Pastor Charles Stanley on the radio the other day, and he said, "The only time we can be absolutely sure about God's will for our lives is yesterday." So why do we see God's purpose in our past with contact lenses and His purpose for our future with cataracts?

Perhaps He has already given us the answer, and we just haven't seen it yet.

Anna and I once attended a youth leaders' conference a few years back, and while we were there, a musician named Kendall Payne performed during one of the sessions. She was a talented singer and songwriter, but the thing I remember most about her was a story she told about a song she had written called "Pray."

In her account, a man was struggling with his purpose in life. He spent years wrestling with what God wanted him to do, and then one day, he decided to do something about it. His goal was simple: He would find Mother Teresa and have her pray for him. He thought if anyone on earth could help him discover how to devote himself fully to God, she could. So he bought a plane ticket to India, and after much searching, he found her at last, ministering to the poor in a slum in Calcutta.

You can imagine the anticipation he felt as he approached her slowly, realizing the moment he had waited for had finally arrived. Kneeling beside her, he drew a deep breath and started a speech he had rehearsed a hundred times. "Mother Teresa, I'm so glad I found you. I traveled all across the world for just this moment. Would you please pray for me?"

She turned toward him, eyes narrowing gently. "Certainly, my dear. How can I pray for you?"

Cheered by the news, he went on. "I want to know what God wants me to do in life. I want clarity about His will for me."

She paused, looking down at the ground, her mouth tightening. "I'm sorry," she said softly, "but I won't pray that for you."

He shifted his feet, pausing a moment longer than normal. "I don't understand. Why not? I just want to serve God with all my heart. I want to minister to others as you have. I want the clarity of purpose you have."

She raised her eyes once more. "My son, I have never had clarity in all my life. I have just learned to obey God each day. But I will pray for you, that you learn to trust and obey Him."

Mother Teresa was pretty legit, and she seems to be on to something there. I think she was saying obedience is the key to purpose in spiritual matters.

If you do a word search in the Bible on *purpose,* you will find something interesting: Scripture doesn't really come right out and tell us our purpose. This hasn't kept theologians from developing ideas about it though. For example, the Westminster Confession of Faith states, "The chief end of man is to glorify God and enjoy Him forever."[8] But this doesn't talk about obedience, so how does this fit in with Mother Teresa's lesson?

I do believe our purpose is to glorify God. I guess I'm wrestling with how to go about doing that. If we figure out how to bring Him glory, and we do whatever it is that brings Him glory, we'll fulfill our purpose, right? I suppose this all depends on whether God will actually reveal to us whatever it is that will bring Him glory.

You'd think He would. After all, "he chose us in him before the foundation of the world, that we should be holy and blameless before him. In love he predestined us for adoption as sons through Jesus Christ, according to the purpose of his will, to the praise of his glorious grace."[9] This fits right alongside that verse you might have wanted to bring up earlier: "For we are his workmanship, created in Christ Jesus for good works, which God prepared beforehand, that we should walk in them."[10]

As hard as this is to understand, God, for His own good reasons and before time even began, seems to have planned for us to become perfect through Jesus, and part of His plan was for us to do these good works He created us to do. And He will somehow get the praise for it all.

Let's be practical for a moment. As I write, I am pretty upset with God because I don't want to do the good works He planned beforehand for me to do right now. I don't even know what the good works are yet, but I know I don't want to do them. I have been agonizing in prayer for months about my purpose, asking God to reveal to me His calling for my life. I even went away on a three-day spiritual retreat to fast and pray for this calling. But I didn't get the big answer I was seeking. The only direction I've received from God since that time is a whole bunch of small circumstances that are leading me somewhere I'd rather not go.

For example, I have been working from home for the past three months, which has been great because I normally travel four days each week for my job, and to be honest, I'm sick of traveling. I've been able to spend a lot of time with Anna and to plug back into Newmen and into the lives of other guys in our community, and I have been refreshed. The arrangement was going so well that I had plans to extend it another six months.

I spoke with one of my partners about it a few days back, and he was in full support, so my future was beginning to take shape. But then I got a call later the same day from another partner who wanted me to work in San Francisco for a few months. I let him know I had requested to work from home, but that didn't seem to faze him. So he ended up putting me on the project anyway, and before I could tell the first partner about it, the deal was done. The worst part of all is that the first partner just sent me a note saying it all happened before he could react; otherwise, he would have been able to do something about it.

So I'm bitter toward God because I feel as if He owes me. I've been on the road for years, and it's time I got a little break from this lifestyle. You might remind me that I chose this job, and you'd be right, but that doesn't make me feel any better at the moment. This time at home has been a great season of intimacy with God, and I've been able to put down roots again and have seen a lot of fruit come from being in town full-time. So I assumed God would just want me to keep producing fruit here.

But He's called me on a mission to Nineveh. And I am following right behind Jonah, spiritually boarding a boat to Tarshish, destined to be thrown overboard and swallowed by a great fish, where I'll pout until I finally come to say, "I called out to the LORD, out of my distress, and he answered me... when my life was fainting away, I remembered the LORD, and my prayer came to you, into your holy temple."[11]

Apparently, part of God making me holy and blameless through Jesus, according to His purpose, is for me to go to San Francisco. He has good works there for me to do, works that will bring Him glory. So when I pray Jonah's prayer, it will be a prayer of surrender to God, and I will be in a place where I can obey Him like Jonah did the next time God called him.[12]

So I find myself learning Mother Teresa's lesson, although slowly and begrudgingly. I asked God to reveal my life's calling to me, and instead, He sent me to San Francisco, which was something I didn't want to do. Simply obeying God is difficult for me because I'd rather do what I want. But although I'm not happy with God, He is my Commander, and He has given me orders, so I'm going to obey. According to the Bible, He must have good works for me to do, so I'm going to go and keep an eye out for them. This means I'm going to have to depend on God, and that's a hard thing to do because it means giving up my own sense of control over my life.

When Paul calls us soldiers of Jesus Christ, I think he is trying to show us what it looks like to give up control over our own lives.[13] After all, soldiers are in the business of obeying orders; in fact, they see that as their purpose. So when Paul goes on to say, "No soldier on service entangles himself in the affairs of life, that he may please him who enrolled him as a soldier," I think he is giving us a vision of how we can live out our lives of faith.[14] Soldiers on duty for Jesus don't allow themselves to get caught up in all the concerns of life, and those who are mired in temporary, worldly pursuits can't be good soldiers.

So Mother Teresa was evidently a good soldier because she learned how to obey orders. I'm sure she wrestled against the "cosmic powers over this present darkness, against the spiritual forces of evil in the heavenly places" as she fought for the dignity of the poor and oppressed in India. I also imagine she took up her shield of faith, strapped on her helmet of salvation, and wielded the sword of the Spirit as she fought her battles for God.[15] But the reason she was a great soldier was because of her simple obedience.

We see the best example of simple, soldierlike obedience in Jesus, and it started before He was even born. Jesus existed in fellowship with God the Father and God the Spirit before time began. He was God, is God, and is the same essence and nature as God. But Jesus as we know Him today—as the God-Man, forever occupying a glorified body—was not always this way. Before He came to earth, He was simply the Word. John tells us, "The Word became flesh and dwelt among us."[16] Why? Because the Father sent Him.[17]

So Jesus entered into humanity as an infant out of obedience to His Father.

We don't get to see much of His life following His birth, but I bet He was a really good kid, helping His mom clear the table after dinner, obeying His father when they were working around the house or in the shop, doing His schoolwork on time, that sort of thing.[18] When the story does catch up with Him at age 12, the year of His bar mitzvah and passage into manhood, we find Him in the temple while His parents searched all of Jerusalem for Him. When they finally found Him, they said, "Son, why have you treated us so? Behold, your father and I have been searching for you in great distress."[19] He calmly replied, "Did you not know that I must be about My Father's business?"[20] The Father must have told the Son about some sort of business because Jesus was going about it, even at the risk of worrying His parents.

So Jesus entered into manhood, staying behind from His family and hanging out at the temple, out of obedience to His Father.

The story has another gap at this point, and all we know is He continued to "increase in wisdom and in stature and in favor with God and man."[21] When the story resumes, Jesus is 30 years old and on His way from Nazareth to the Jordan River.[22] He had spent most of His life working as a carpenter in the small town of Nazareth, but now He had left his home, family, and friends. He must have done so, not on a whim, but as a result of His Father's direction.

So Jesus entered into ministry out of obedience to His Father.

This pattern continued for the rest of Jesus' ministry. After He was baptized, He was led by the Spirit into the wilderness to be tempted, and He went.[23] When he spoke to the Samaritan woman at the well, and His disciples came and found Him weary and urged Him to eat, He said, "My food is to do the will of him who sent me and to accomplish his work."[24] One time He told the crowds that followed Him, "I have come down from heaven, not to do my own will but the will of him who sent me."[25] Another time,

He spoke to the Pharisees and told them, "I can do nothing on my own. I judge as God tells me."[26] And in perhaps the most explicit declaration of His dependence on God, He said, "Truly, truly, I say to you, the Son can do nothing of his own accord, but only what he sees the Father doing. For whatever the Father does, that the Son does likewise."[27]

Evidently then, time after time, on occasion after occasion, throughout the balance of His life that is known to us, Jesus continued to do only what His Father told Him to do. This does not quite make sense because He was and is God, so He should already have known where to go and what to do. But in evidencing His full humanity, He seemed to draw solely from the will of His Father. Maybe this is why He prayed so much—He was asking the Father what He should do next.[28] When His Father spoke, He obeyed. He had been given all authority, and yet He did only what His Father told Him. In all this, Jesus seemed to be interested most in simple obedience.

I'd love to call Jesus a good soldier like Mother Teresa because of His commitment to obedience, but it's kind of His army after all. So I'll just say He demonstrated perfect obedience, and I think He did so because He wanted to show us how love flows between God and man.

When we explored the reason for God's rules in the last chapter, we saw they existed to show our sin and to point to grace, and although our obedience to Jesus' commands doesn't make God love us more, it does create space for intimacy with Him. That's all fine and well, but how does that relate to Jesus' obedience and our purpose?

Here's how I see it. Grace is useful only when there's an undeserving person who receives it. And obedience works only if there's a superior person to be obeyed. Both act as channels for love to flow between God, the superior person to be obeyed, and man, the undeserving person in need of grace. To put it another way, God shows us love through grace, and we show God love through obedience. Or if we want to use the analogy of the vine we saw in the last chapter, God's grace grafts our branch into the vine of Jesus, and our obedience, by the power of His grace, maintains that union so His love can flow through us, both down to us and back up to Him, which in turn produces fruit for the glory of God.

Jesus demonstrated this for us. He was able to love God perfectly because He obeyed God perfectly. And He was the only one who could have shown us these two channels for love because He has been both greater, as God and the source of grace, and lesser, as a man who, although God, could say in truth, "The Father is greater than I."[29]

If this is true, then my desire to know my whole life's purpose so I can set out on my own to fulfill it without having to obey God each day becomes a traitor in the ranks. The purpose of our lives, to glorify God, is fulfilled through our love-filled obedience; they're not things to be sought after separately.

You may be asking the same question I just asked myself. *That's all very interesting, but what does this have to do with my life?*

I can only tell you what it means for me, but perhaps you can relate. I'm kind of an achiever; I have large dreams and a lot of motivation. I want to be successful in my job, and I want to have a good family with smart, obedient kids. I want to have a nice enough house, and I want to go on interesting vacations. I want to be liked by my coworkers and friends and be respected by the people in my church.

I even have spiritual ambitions; I want to accomplish great things for the Lord. I want to do my part to advance His kingdom on earth, reaching hundreds or thousands or tens of thousands of people for Jesus. I want to have an impact on their souls, to have the vapor that is my life count for something greater than me. I want to do my part to declare God's glory to the nations, to spread a passion for the supremacy of Christ in all things.[30] I want to spend my life on Christ so that when I come before Him in judgment, I will hear, "Well done, good and faithful servant."

I'm sure you've noticed the refrain: "I want."

But this attitude is the opposite of simple obedience. It is not the mantra of the soldier. Simple, soldierlike obedience is about what God wants, not what we want. Some of those desires are not bad things; in fact, some are noble and God-honoring. The problem is that I get focused on them, so if God doesn't mean for me to glorify Him in those ways, I'm not content. Do I care enough about the glory of God that I would be satisfied to be used in small ways to bring Him glory? Not yet.

I've also realized this kind of ambition is born out of my desire to know my purpose in life rather than to glorify God through simple, soldierlike obedience. My cravings for more of God have led me down a path of wanting to do more for God rather than wanting to know more of God.

This is why I need to go back to boot camp, and if you find yourself either not caring enough about God's glory or caring too much about how great you are going to be for God, perhaps you need to join me as well. There we'll leave our own lives behind, shave our spiritual heads, put on the uniform of Christ, and learn to march in step while the Holy Spirit calls out cadence. And over time, our desires as individuals will weaken and will be replaced by the growing bonds of love for the civilians (the lost), the unit (the church), the Commander (Jesus), and the mission (glorifying God).

This will be exactly what we need because our eyes will be opened to the global redemptive story of God in our world, and we'll remember that Jesus is the star and that all things exist for Him.[31] And we'll be able to find our individual, local mission as part of that larger story. We won't even think about deserting, because we will love and obey our Commander. After all, He first loved us enough to give His own life for us on the field of battle.

So when we struggle with our purpose in life, my encouragement to you and reminder to myself is not to exhaust our spirits in anxious anticipation of tomorrow, but to put on the uniform of a soldier of Christ and do what Jesus did instead:

Ask God what to do next.

11. Child:

Why We Must
Act like Children

I want to be 12 years old again.

Until recently, I have always acted above my age. When I was in the third grade at my all-boy Christian grade school, I was selected as a Crusader, which was a position of responsibility for students with leadership potential. At least they told us it was a position of responsibility; all I remember doing was taking notes from teachers to the office. But I took the job and my schoolwork seriously.

In fact, the only time I got in trouble in grade school was during a fire drill. Whenever the fire alarm rang, we were supposed to quickly and silently move in single file out the door of our classroom, down the hallway and staircase, and out to the lawn. Talking was prohibited. But one day during a fire drill, as my class filed down the stairwell, I heard the boy in front of me whisper something to the boy in front of him. I quietly said, "Hey, we're not allowed to talk," thinking I was performing my duty as a Crusader to keep order and discipline in the ranks.

But that is when one of the teachers came through the door at the top of the stairs. I could feel her presence, her body backlit by the light of the hallway. She had heard my whisper, and she had caught me in the act. She told my favorite teacher, Miss Maddox, what I had done. I tried to explain myself, but Miss Maddox put my name in her black book and sent me home with a Misconduct Slip. I thought my life had ended at that moment, and when I got home, I burst into tears and told my mom I was never going back to school again.

I lived out my youth in a kind of tension, secretly wanting to be normal and cool and all the things I suppose most kids care about, but also desiring something more, constantly being drawn to the serious side of life. This tension grew in junior high, where I finally had something else to be serious about besides school and sports: girls.

I quickly found my first girlfriend, Nicole, who I thought was amazing. Nicole was pretty and popular, and I was serious about her. I bought her $40 earrings from Sears because I wanted her to know I was committed to our relationship, even at the age of 12. When her friend called me a week later to tell me Nicole didn't want to go out anymore because we didn't go on enough dates, I was crushed.

As I ended my junior high career, I took my gravity into the spiritual realm, receiving the Timothy Award, given to the student who most displays Christian behavior, as I left eighth grade. Maybe it had to do with the fact that I was kind of boring, and sometimes boring people seem spiritual. I actually don't recall this event, but I bet it was satisfying to a young teenager who always desired respect. My mom swears I was embarrassed by the whole thing and that I started acting up a bit more from that point onward, but I think she's reaching.

After all, just about the worst thing I did in high school was a nighttime attack on a guy's house with my buddies David and Frazer. We donned black outfits and ski masks and spread thousands of paper shreds throughout his parents' flower garden. We also TPed his trees, stuck hundreds of plastic forks in his lawn, although I'm not sure why, and smeared Vaseline on his windshield, which must have taken hours to clean off. But the *pièce de résistance* was our secret weapon: a six-month-old piece of rotting chicken Frazer had been saving in the freezer in his garage. It was enclosed in two quart-sized ziplock bags, but it still stunk so bad we had to drive with it hanging out the window. As our final act of terror, we stuck that nasty chicken into the rear bumper of this guy's car so he'd smell the stench but not be able to find it.

But even all of this wasn't because we were mean kids or didn't like this guy. He was a friend, and we did it because the three of us were collectively paid $400 by another friend who was mad at him. So even when I misbehaved, I exhibited deliberate planning and professional interest.

When I wasn't selling out my serious look on life for $133, I continued adding bullets to my budding high school résumé. I was elected as a class officer my junior and senior years, winning those positions with the thrilling slogan created by my friend Amy: "Don't Miss—Vote for Chris!" I got good grades, behaved in class, joined the Bible Club, played sports, and looked down on all my friends who acted as if adolescence was supposed to be fun.

College was no different. Instead of choosing a normal school where I could go to have a good time, I chose the U.S. Air Force Academy, where I could march to breakfast. Some of my Academy friends did their fair share of goofing off, and while I occasionally joined them, I was more often interested in serious things like leadership positions. And since graduating from college and heading off to business school, I've done nothing but become an even more serious adult.

Forgive me for sharing my résumé, but the point is that I'm way too serious, and I've been acting like an adult as long as I can remember, and it's not exactly something I'd like to be. I've often wanted to have more fun, or more accurately, to be more fun, but this is how I find myself. So when I say I want to be 12 years old again, I'm going against the full evidence of my life.

Thank God for friends. I have three friends in particular, Rillos, Zitz, and Erik, who are total clowns. They are all solid men, ex–Air Force, successful in their careers, and fathers. But these guys act like complete idiots pretty much any time we are all together, and their example, if you want to call it that, has done wonders for me in shedding some of my seriousness.

Rillos and Erik once did a monthlong analysis of the bathroom stall usage at their Air Force office so they could determine the ones that were least used and therefore most sanitary. Another time Erik climbed on top of Rillos' roof at a Fourth of July party to do lunges in his Speedo. I used to catch Zitz in his office trying to stand on an exercise ball, at times while throwing pencils into the ceiling tiles so they'd stick. And I'll never forget the time the three of us pulled up to one of our favorite surf spots, and while I was waxing my board, I looked over to find one of them, and I won't say whom, relieving himself on my truck's rear tire.

Whenever I see another one of their wrestling matches in public, I have an urge to release my inner child, to make a fool of myself alongside them, and to shed my shroud of seriousness. Most of the time I don't, but I still want to act like a little kid because kids seem to have a lot more fun than I do.

Maybe this is why I joined our church's youth group. I signed up to be a junior high leader, and one of the job qualifications is the ability to make a fool of yourself at any time. On long bus trips, I'd get into wrestling matches with the boys in the back, or they'd talk me into yelling at them like a drill sergeant so they could pretend they were in the military. Once I led a coordinated land and naval assault on the high schoolers' houseboats, half the boys lobbing oranges from the nearby shore while a few of us hurled leftover food from atop the decks of our waverunners.

As much as I liked acting like a kid with these students, I still retained my sober-minded seriousness most of the time. My inner child and my outer adult engaged in a constant wrestling match, although it wasn't much of a contest because my outer adult pummeled my inner child most of the time. On rare occasions, something happened that sent the outer adult screaming from the mat, and all that was left was the inner child, confused and alone.

One such occasion happened during a winter camp at Big Bear Mountain. Anna and I had spent the day snowboarding with the kids, and we were all driving partway down the mountain to our camp. I was driving the equipment van, and Anna was behind me in our truck. The first half of the drive was uneventful as a gentle snow began to fall. Uneventful, that is, until cars started sliding off the road.

The first to go was our cargo truck, slipping into a shallow ditch and slamming into a snow embankment. Anna followed suit in our truck. I quickly pulled the van over and ran back to her, seeing panic and fear in her eyes. I stuck my head inside the vehicle to make sure the girls in the backseat were all right, and although no one was hurt, they looked pretty scared too.

To be honest, I was scared as well because I didn't know what we were going to do. Part of me just wanted to be like a little kid again, to have my mom or dad take care of everything. But I could tell that Anna and her girls were worried, and I knew I had to be the serious one. So I assessed the problem and gave a few directions to Anna, her girls, and some of my boys.

Anna and I began the long process of trying to fix our dilemma. We started digging out all the snow around my truck, looking for rocks or sticks to put under the tires, trying to find something for the wheels to grasp. But nothing was working. We continued to dig, and we kept trying to drive the trucks out of the ditch, but it quickly became a lost cause. Things got a little scarier quickly when a Jeep and a minivan slid off the road in the same spot, one of them hitting my truck in the ditch.

Half an hour into this ordeal, with the snow continuing to fall and the cold seeping into the bones of my bare hands, I finally turned to what should have been my first response: prayer. I don't know why I didn't think of it first. Actually, I do know—this is typical for me. A 12-year-old boy who is scared runs to his father for help. But a serious adult has no time for that; he has problems to solve here and now, and time is of the essence.

So I asked the girls in the truck to begin praying, although I think they were already doing so. Hearing little-girl prayers for safety and rescue reminded me what it feels like to be afraid like a child, to not be able to do anything other than reach out to God for help. That's when I remembered our snow chains, and my outer adult came back to life.

The chains were too big for my truck, but that didn't mean we couldn't lay them on the ground for the tires to grip as I drove out of the ditch. So that's what we did; I sent one of the students back to the van as Anna and I cleared a space in front of each tire. When Mac returned with the chains, we laid them out flat, arcing them toward the road, leading the tires on the path to freedom.

As I jumped into the driver's seat, I felt sure this was going to work. I put the truck in 4-wheel low, popped the emergency brake, and shifted into drive. The wheels caught metal in a welcome embrace, and the truck lurched forward. We were back on the road!

This would have been great—if we had stayed on the road. But the road was too slick and our truck too heavy, and it slid once more back into the ditch. The problem was now worse because instead of sitting long-ways in the ditch, we were suddenly perpendicular to the road with half of my truck sticking into the right lane of a mountain road covered in ice. The little girls started praying again, asking God to help us. My outer adult ran helplessly from the mat, and my inner child just lay there, crying for help or mother or God or anything.

But I serve a God who is in control of all things, who knows the details of every problem I encounter and the depth of every ditch I get stuck in. In these times, He walks lovingly onto the mat, picking up my inner child gently and whispering that everything is going to be all right. God has the answer to my every problem, and He sometimes proves even more useful than snow chains.

God rescued us, and He did so in the form of a monster truck, complete with a dirt bike strapped to the truck bed. Trucks like that one don't come equipped with air fresheners and heated seats; they come standard with big, thick tow ropes strong enough to pull two trucks from the clutches of a car-eating ditch. The crisis, which felt like it lasted for hours, was resolved in minutes, and we were soon on the road and on our way down the mountain, my confidence growing with each turn of our wheels and my whimpering child giving way to the resolute man inside. We made our way to camp and gave God praise for delivering us safely, but the lesson had only begun.

Anna and I snuck out from our cabins that night to talk about the evening's drama, and while I was gone, the boys in my cabin broke a window in the cabin next door, but that is a different story. We sat in my truck and had a good conversation, sorting through the events of the night and seeing with contact-lens vision that God had been in control all along.

Anna had been courageous during the crisis, summoning her own outer adult in spite of her fear, but she shared that she had been scared for most of the evening, and she felt as if she hadn't displayed much faith in God. Neither had I. While the girls in the backseat of our truck were turning to God with simple pleas for help, Anna and I were out trying to solve the problem on our own. The more we talked that night, the more I realized we were both struggling with the reason everything had happened, wanting to be able to explain the night's events so we could feel in control of the situation.

Anna wanted answers, and I did too. I find myself thinking these kinds of thoughts regularly. As you might have noticed, I believe God is involved in the smallest details of our lives, so I am always searching for the meaning behind everything, trying to reason through people's behaviors or a turn of events, searching for His purpose that sits just beneath the surface of life. I cannot accept life for what it appears to be because my serious nature wants to know more. This is what outer adults do; they demand an explanation.

But God doesn't seem to want me to know every detail about how the world works, and He doesn't often cater to my demands for an explanation. In fact, He seems to conceal much of His hand in my life. You may have found the same to be true in your life as well. He must delight in this sense of mystery because it reveals something about Him that is worth knowing and something about us that is worth understanding. And I imagine this is where part of our craving for more of Him arises, from this desire to resolve the mystery we feel when we think about God.

As Christians, we attend a lot of churches, read a lot of books, go to a lot of Bible studies, listen to a lot of Christian music, and believe we know a lot about this God we worship. But if we were to be honest with each other, and we thought long and hard about our beliefs and our questions, we'd probably admit we just don't understand quite a bit about God, and I don't know that this will ever change. All of eternity won't be enough time for us to fully comprehend the infinite glory of God.

If you're like me, you may find statements about the infinite glory of God to be vague, and as a consequence, you may be in the habit of reducing God to something you can understand. God becomes harsh like a tyrant, or loving like a Father, or fair like a judge, or giving like Santa Claus, or anything like anything. The point is we think God is *like* something.

But we shouldn't beat ourselves up about it, because God describes Himself as Father and Friend and other sorts of things. I imagine He does so because He is so different, and the only way we can begin to understand Him is to think of Him like something we do understand.[1] The problem is when we think that is *all* God is like.

God is really only like God. He is incomparable, so calling Him like anything doesn't do Him justice. Paul wraps up his doctrinal dissertation in Romans by saying, "Oh, the depth of the riches and wisdom and knowledge of God! How unsearchable are his judgments and how inscrutable his ways!"[2] The moment He reveals Himself in shining glory is the moment before He is hidden from our sight once more.

So God reveals parts of Himself to us in creation, in our consciences, or through His Word, but He leaves much unexplained.[3] And that's just not good enough for my adultlike, serious perspective. When my outer adult gets used to beating down my inner child, he begins to think he's pretty special and starts to question more than should be questioned, which always leads to trouble.

As you saw from my résumé, my life has been a nearly uninterrupted string of serious, outer-adult pursuits, and my faith is no different. This may be the same thing as saying my faith is cynical. I seek rational explanations for the movement of God in my life and in the world rather than accepting them and celebrating them as evidence of His power.

Once Anna and I were in Burkina Faso, West Africa, on a mission trip with our friends, and we were participating in a time of prayer and worship at the orphan center with 60 or so widows from the village. Part of the tradition in those meeting times is to share testimonies, but these are not the life-story testimonies we typically hear in the West. These are testimonies like, "My child was sick last week, and God healed him." During this time of testimony, one widow near the back of the room stood up and testified that she had come to the meeting as a blind woman, and she could now see. Instead of doing what a kid would have done, which would have been to clap in praise to God, I wanted to ask for medical records.

Another time I was struggling with questions about the future (not yet embracing my purpose in glorifying God through simple obedience), and I had been praying for God to open doors for Anna and me. One evening during this time, we were coming back from a birthday party for my friend Tim, and we found our front door locked. So I boosted Anna up to our 12-foot-high balcony to see if the patio door was locked, which it was. We were both bummed because she was stuck up there and I was going to have to pay a locksmith a hundred bucks to open our door. While I was going to borrow a phone, Anna tried to open the door a few more times, and we both started praying, and all of a sudden, the door was open. Again, instead of doing what a kid would have done, which would have been to run around the house laughing at God's sense of humor, I walked in the house and examined the lock to see how it could possibly have opened.

Adults ask for medical records; children smile and clap. Adults examine locks; children laugh and run around the house.

Maybe this is why Jesus said, "Truly, I say to you, whoever does not receive the kingdom of God like a child shall not enter it."[4] Jesus seemed to be highlighting an important difference between receiving the kingdom of God like a child and receiving the kingdom like an adult: One works, and the other doesn't.

Little children receive undeserved gifts with joy and without reservation because they don't know enough to know they don't deserve them. Adults can never accept such gifts in the same way. They have too much shame or too much pride.[5]

Having childlike faith means accepting God's gift of grace with joy and without reservation.[6] If we try to receive Jesus like an adult, we will either end up rejecting Him because we have too much shame or we'll turn His gift into a religion to try to pay Him back. Of course, both children and adults can receive Jesus like a child, but neither can receive Him like an adult.

Perhaps most of all, children have a much greater capacity for awe than do adults, so childlike faith bears a sense of amazement in receiving such a gift. Awe can come from fear, which is the beginning of wisdom, or it can come from wonder, which is the beginning of worship.[7] So awe turns our focus from ourselves to God, from the gift to the Giver.

Nothing makes me feel quite so small as thinking about the creation of the universe. Quiet your heart for a moment and allow your mind to expand into the darkness of space, journeying back in time through the torrential rush of everything that fills our expanding universe. Imagine the material nothingness that existed a split second before all of creation exploded into being. Think about the moment in time, if we can even call it that, when the fullness of God's creative power was unleashed in a word. Dwell there, pausing to consider where God was before that moment of creation.

And then think back to where God was before that moment. And before that.

Stretch your mind back through your life, through the lives of your parents, and their parents, and their parents, and all their ancestors throughout history; through the first steps of Adam upon softened soil, or the flight or movement of every kind of bird and animal and sea creature and plant;

through the jolting rise of land out of frothing seas, through the crack of air splitting from water, through the burst of millions of stars into darkness, through creation itself, and find where God starts.

My head begins to hurt when I do this. Arriving at God's beginning is like catching sound in your hand or describing color to the blind. Job's friend, Zophar, asks us, "Can you solve the mysteries of God? Can you discover everything about the Almighty?"[8] The prophet Isaiah, in a profound state of awe and wonder, says, "Truly, O God…you work in mysterious ways."[9]

We experience a certain kind of awe when we contemplate God's existence before time began, and we sense another kind of awe when we realize God is bringing a monster truck to help us out of an icy ditch. Both kinds of awe lead us closer to God, and they remind us He is in control and He is in charge. They remind us we don't have to be the adults who wrestle alone with our problems in life. We have a Father who can beat down any opponent that gets in our face.

When you and I left boot camp marching in step with the call of the Spirit, our posture as soldiers was one of simple obedience. I think we're finding that the posture of a soldier is not that different from the posture of a child. Soldiers recognize and respect authority, as do children. Good soldiers will obey their commanders, and good children will obey their parents. Maybe this is why Peter calls us "obedient children."[10]

But childlike faith adds something that a soldierlike, outward, adult kind of faith can lack: joy.

This is why I want to be 12 years old again. I want to obey like a soldier so I can bring God glory, but I also want to receive like a child so I can find joy in doing it. I want to remember the feeling of being a child who is sitting in the back of a truck that is stuck in the snow and praying to God to save me instead of being the adult who is frantically sticking rocks under the tires of the truck, trying to save myself. I want to figure out the spiritual equivalent to standing on an exercise ball and throwing pencils at the ceiling and do that, because faith was meant to be fun, not just serious.

The child's perspective on joy is a powerful image, and no one does it more justice than C.S. Lewis in *The Chronicles of Narnia: The Last Battle*. In this treatment of the end times, Lewis gives us a glimpse into the mind of a child overwhelmed by the security and joy in Jesus. Aslan, Lewis' representation of Christ, commands the end of the world and gathers all those who sought and knew Him. Accompanying Aslan are the noble characters of Narnia's past, including the faun Tumnus and the old kings and queens of Narnia: Peter, Edmund, and the youngest, Lucy. Upon her arrival in the atrium of heaven, Lucy was noted as "drinking everything in more deeply than the others. She had been too happy to speak."[11]

Lucy drank everything in more deeply than the others because her focus was on Aslan. Throughout her adventures in Narnia, she was always the one who longed to see Him most. While the others were marveling at their extraordinary surroundings, her simple, childlike faith and her longing to see her King brought her speechless joy.

For most of us, our outer adults ask far too many questions and rely far too often on their own strength to be able to deeply drink in everything the way Lucy did. What would it be like to be children once more, to think big thoughts about God instead of worrying about our retirement accounts? And what would our lives look like if we reacquainted ourselves with our inner children, going to God first when we're in need of help? The place we automatically go the moment we're in trouble is a good indicator of whom we trust the most. Far too often, I turn first to myself, and then maybe to family and close friends, but God is typically third or fourth at best.

But I bet Lucy would go to Aslan first. I imagine her cravings to see Him and have Him rescue her in her time of need are born out of her childlike faith. And this kind of faith awakens a desire for more of the grandness of God. When we want more of God, we long to heed Aslan's call to "Come further in! Come further up!"[12] And Tumnus tells us why: "The further up and the further in you go, the bigger everything gets."[13]

This is why I want to be 12 years old again—because to a child, everything is big.

Especially God.

12. Hunger:

What Hunger
Teaches Us About God

I once knew a guy who talked about food all day long for eight days straight.

He talked about cheeseburgers and fries and pizza. He spoke about meat loaf and mashed potatoes and macaroni and cheese and green beans and cornbread. He dreamed about ravioli with lasagna piled on top and a side of garlic bread. He drooled over thoughts of chocolate and cinnamon rolls and ice cream. He relished thoughts about every kind of good food a person could possibly want.

He went about his days, doing the things he was supposed to do, but all of his focus was on food. Day after day, even during the night sometimes, whether walking or sitting or standing, he just kept talking about food. It occupied his thoughts and his words; it utterly consumed him to the point where nothing mattered in the entire world except food.

That guy was me. And I was really hungry.

I graduated from the United States Air Force Academy with the Class of 2000. During the summer of 1997, I, along with a thousand of my classmates, went through Combat Survival Training (CST). The purpose of CST was to teach us how to survive and evade capture should we find ourselves in hostile territory during wartime, which was taxpayer money well spent on a future space systems program manager in California.

CST was the most dreaded time in every upperclassman's cadet career. It was mandatory for all cadets to complete in order to graduate, so we had no choice, and we knew we wouldn't eat much while out in the field as that was part of the training environment. The first half of field training was called Survival, so we constructed our tents and learned to make fires and practiced finding and decontaminating water sources and that sort of thing. I don't know if you've ever had the chance to drink muddy water, but it doesn't taste very good. We were taught how to strain the water so that it would become less muddy, and we were given iodine pills to make it potable, but iodine-flavored, faintly muddy water isn't that much better than plain muddy water, and it doesn't do much for hunger either.

The second half of field training was called Evasion. Our task was to navigate, in teams of three, several miles through the woods and mountains, using only our compasses, maps, and knotted rope. Each night, we were expected to find our way to one of four waypoints, crossing several miles of mountain forest while moving slowly and quietly enough to evade capture from the scores of cadre who were sent out to catch anyone they could find.

At each waypoint, we faced simulated allies who were kind to us or enemies who were harsh. Some of the waypoints were easy to find, others harder, but all the while, our hunger was driving us crazy. Our group ended up making our way through all four waypoints, and we even did well enough to score a helicopter ride home rather than a bus ride with most of the other cadets. Getting back to the academy felt great after a week in the woods, as did a shower and a bed, even one with hospital-cornered sheets.

But what I longed for the most was food. After 45 minutes of scrubbing in the shower, desperately trying to get the camouflage and dirt off my hands, head, neck, eyelids, and ears, I headed back to my room, where I dialed up a local Italian place for delivery. I decided to start small: just a large pizza and a plate of ravioli. I figured I could get to the cheeseburger and ice cream later.

The next 30 minutes felt like a lifetime. I don't know the feeling of watching the birth of your first child, having waited anxiously for nine months and dreamed day and night about the upcoming moment, but I bet it feels a little bit the same way I did when the delivery guy showed up at our stairwell. I paid him and tipped him well. I may have even hugged him.

The first bite was amazing, and relief washed over me. The next bite was even better, my taste buds coming to life and savoring every moment. But the third bite brought a different sensation. It was neither relief nor pleasure; it was the feeling of being full. I had not eaten any substantial food in weeks, my stomach had downsized, and I could no longer eat anything close to a full meal. I wanted more, but at the same time, I didn't. My hunger was satisfied with the smallest amount of food.

My CST experience is now in the past, and I hadn't thought about it much until recently when I read a book that brought back a lot of these memories. The book is called *The Heavenly Man,* and it is the true story of a man named Brother Yun, who was one of the leaders of the house-church movement in China in the last 30 years.

During the course of his life, Yun was imprisoned on many occasions for preaching the gospel, and he suffered beatings, ridicule, and all sorts of torturous and demeaning acts. His prison time sounds horrible, but his story of going on a food strike is the most amazing. While Yun was in prison in Nanyang in 1984, he sensed the Lord calling him to fast. He used his time of fasting to seek God, but the prison authorities took it as a sign of rebellion, so they continued to beat and torture him. Yet in spite of his harsh treatment, he persisted in his fast. Days turned into weeks, and his fast was unbroken, as was the torture. His body grew weaker, but he felt more and more sustained by God, so he continued to fast.

He soon approached the thirty-ninth day of his fast, and he was nearly overcome with temptation by the devil. Jesus had fasted for 40 days, so surely Yun would not presume to try and surpass his Lord in this fast. But God seemed to be calling him to persevere, so he persisted in his refusal of food. Soon he approached the fiftieth day of the fast. Then the sixtieth. Then the seventieth day.

By the seventy-fourth day, the prison authorities had exhausted all of their disciplinary techniques on Yun, and in their haste to bring his fast to an end, they arranged for his family to come see him, hoping they would convince him to finally eat. His family was brought into a room, and a cellmate carried Yun to see them because Yun was far too weak at that point to move anywhere by himself. At first, his family didn't recognize him. But then his mother identified his birthmark, and his family soon faced the fact that the shrunken and shriveled body that lay before them was their beloved Yun.

Brother Yun's wife, Deling, recounts seeing her husband at the end of his fast:

> After some time a tiny figure was carried in…he looked like a little child [because he had dropped from 165 pounds to 65]…he was so little that he didn't even look like a human being. Most of his hair had been torn out. His face was gaunt. His eyes appeared larger than normal, and his mouth hung open, displaying yellow teeth.[1]

I don't know if you have ever seen a picture of someone in this condition, but I'm sure it's a stark image. The human body is frail, and it doesn't take too many days without nourishment to show its weakness. I can't imagine the feeling of seeing this strong, virtuous man reduced to nothing more than tightly stretched skin over beaten, bruised bones.

As I tried to imagine myself as Yun's mother or wife, eyes scanning across this shriveled form of a man, I remembered CST. I lost 20 pounds during training, not 100, but I didn't exactly have 20 pounds to lose. My skin stretched more tightly across my ribs; some of my already scarce muscle mass disappeared altogether. I was a picture of relative malnourishment, and while I was nowhere near the condition Yun had been in, my body was still in obvious need of sustenance.

But then my thoughts turned inward. I wondered what my spirit would look like if I could see its health. Would it appear strong and vigorous, filled with the power of God, or would it appear weak and shriveled, evidencing a lack of spiritual nourishment?

Of course, I have no idea what my spirit looks like because I can't see it. I would like to think my spirit is ridiculously ripped, that it is tall and strapping, moving with purpose and the subtle weight of authority. I'd like to believe my spirit always has facial hair and smells like sawdust or fresh dirt because that's what manly spirits are like, right?

Most likely, my spirit is not ridiculously ripped, but ridiculously skinny. I bet it's small and frail, bent over by the torture of a thousand cares and emaciated from lack of any true nourishment. For much of my life, I have eaten some spiritual food, never really starving myself to death but never really feasting either. On the rare occasion my spirit does feast, I too quickly forget the feeling of satisfaction and go back to table scraps. But feasts and scraps aside, the point is I just don't know what my spirit looks like.

Thinking about what my spirit might look like reminded me of the day I met Cal after a surf session in Manhattan Beach on a Tuesday morning. Cal had been living on the beach for many years, and he was in need of good conversation. He's a smart guy, very friendly, and in pretty good shape. He was a little more than 50 years old at the time, with a tanned complexion and a cloud-white beard. But living on the beach doesn't give a man the opportunity to clean up too much. So one afternoon, I invited him up to my apartment for a shave and a shower. He headed into the bathroom armed with a small pair of scissors, a bottle of shaving cream, a razor, and a towel. I didn't see him again for two hours.

When he finally came out, he looked much happier. He also looked good; his beard was trimmed, his hair was combed neatly, and he had a big smile on his face.

"You look good, Cal," I said.

"It's crazy. I hardly recognize myself," he replied, shaking his head. "I haven't looked at myself in a mirror in a long time. These eyes are not the eyes I remember. My hair and beard don't look like I remember. My skin looks different too."

Hearing Cal's perspective got me thinking. I've never forgotten what I look like because I look in a mirror at least once a day. If I think of the times I've been camping or something like that, I'd say the longest I've gone without seeing my own reflection has been a couple of days. So I can't imagine what it feels like to see myself as I am and not recognize the person I see. The experience is probably a little scary and a little confusing. I bet I would just stare, trying to wrestle with the fact that I'm not the person I thought I was.

What Cal lacked was the opportunity to see himself on a regular basis, and it caused him to lose sight of who he was. I wondered if my inability to see my spirit on a regular basis had a similar effect on my own vision.

Fortunately, Jesus had something to say on this subject: "Woe to you, teachers of the law and Pharisees, you hypocrites! You clean the outside of the cup and dish, but inside they are full of greed and self-indulgence. Blind Pharisee! First clean the inside of the cup and dish, and then the outside also will be clean."[2]

These Pharisees thought they were the picture of spiritual health. They followed all of the customs and rules of their religion, even to the smallest degree. They were the keepers of the sacred text, the teachers of God's law for their people. They gave generously (and publicly), prayed fervently (and publicly), and fasted regularly (and publicly). Everyone in town knew these guys were spiritual; if you wanted to be spiritual too, you needed to be like the Pharisees.

Jesus, however, called them filthy, and He also distinguished between two kinds of clean. The first kind of clean ("you clean the outside of the cup") is a superficial kind, like putting a coat of paint over a mold-infested wall. The second kind of clean ("first clean the inside of the cup and dish, and then the outside also will be clean") is a deeper kind. It would require tearing down the wall, killing all the mold, and putting up a new wall in its place. Jesus told the Pharisees that their spiritual health was malnourished and that if they wanted true nourishment, they needed to turn inward first.

But Jesus said something else here as well—He called these Pharisees blind. He didn't just call them filthy. He called them filthy *and* told them they couldn't even see they were filthy. But these Pharisees weren't physically blind, so Jesus must have meant they couldn't see their true spiritual condition. They couldn't see themselves as Jesus saw them.

Whenever I read about the Pharisees, I always imagine them as misguided and ritualistic legalists. I rarely identify with them. But you have learned a little bit about me, and you may have noticed some of my Pharisaical tendencies, some of the legalism that has been hanging out on my couch for many years, and some of my tendency to take hold of some good commandment of God and make it my religion. I am far more like the Pharisees than I care to admit, so I wondered if I was blind to the same thing they were. Do I clean the outside of my cup, learning to say the right words with my friends or measure my level of spirituality by what I do, all the while being blind to the filth on the inside?

I turned to the Scriptures, hoping to regain my sight, and I saw some pretty interesting things. One of the things I noticed was that the Old Testament promised that God would heal the blind.[3] It doesn't say He would heal every blind person; it just says that God is the one who would heal the blind.

You likely remember some of the stories of Jesus healing blind people. Two blind shouters outside the city of Jericho cried out for mercy from the Son of David.[4] Two blind followers tracked Jesus down in a house and were healed.[5] And when a mute and blind demoniac met Jesus, he ended up talking and seeing. In this last account, Matthew introduces this story by quoting from the prophet Isaiah, opening with the promise about God's chosen servant who, among other things, would "open the eyes that are blind."[6]

So the prophets promised God would heal the blind, and Jesus came and did just that. I don't need to convince you that Jesus is God, but I think His role in our ability to see is crucial if we're ever going to see ourselves as we truly are.

If God is the one who opens the eyes of the blind, then the reason the Pharisees were blind seems to be that He had not opened their eyes to see. Jesus' admonishment to them to clean the inside of their cup was, in part, a call to faith, a call to believe in Him. So even though I feared that I might be blind as well, sharing the company of these Pharisees, I realized that by God's grace, I am not. I know God has granted me sight, having given me the gift of Jesus' righteousness and His Spirit to live within me.

John Newton's words echo the chorus of my heart: "I once was lost but now am found, was blind but now I see." I know I have the eyes to see my own filth; I just need God's help to focus and start cleaning.

So I'm somewhat relieved to know I am not blind in the same way the Pharisees were, but this still doesn't help with the fact that I don't really know how healthy my spirit is. Maybe you feel the same way. You know God is for you and you are His because you know the inside of your cup is filthy. I think knowing this is the beginning of seeing yourself as God sees you. It's the staring at yourself in a mirror, as Cal did, and knowing the person you see is you even though the reflection isn't always pretty.

This is where Jesus' picture of the cup is so useful. A cup is meant to hold things. A cup that holds nothing falls short in its true cupness. Perhaps our lives are much the same way. We are all spiritual beings, which means we're all born with a spirit, that something inside us that we know is the real us and not just the outer shell of our body. If, as Jesus said, we are cups, and we hold nothing spiritually, then we fall short of being who we're supposed to be.

But none of us are empty. We all fill our cups with something.

Because we can't see our spirits, we have to rely on something else to give us a vision of our spiritual health. I think this is where our cravings are so instructive. They tell us what we're hungering for, what we're trying to fill our cups with.

Some of us fill our cups with food, believing that a bad day melts away with a bit of chocolate. Others of us fill our cups with sex, thinking that physical intimacy is the way to feel the love and acceptance we long for. Still others search after significance, supposing a job or career will satisfy our deepest longings for purpose and meaning. Committed Christians often fill their cups with religion and rules.

But none of the things we crave, whether food, sex, a career, religion, or anything else in this world, can fill a spiritual cup made for spiritual filling. In fact, any of these counterfeits will make us sick—so sick, in fact, that we will fall into bondage to them and come to hate them.

To see that this is true, we can look at the story of the Exodus from Egypt. In the Bible, Egypt often represents bondage, and God's deliverance of His people out of Egypt is a story of rescue from bondage. God did all sorts of amazing things during this rescue mission: He turned the Nile to blood, sent plague after plague on the Egyptians while protecting the Israelites among them from each one, plundered the Egyptians as His people were freed, parted the Red Sea so Israel could cross on dry land, destroyed Pharoah's army when it was in pursuit, and even fed the people with manna, or bread from heaven, as they crossed the wilderness.[7]

As good as bread from heaven may sound, the people got tired of it pretty quickly. "Now the rabble that was among them had a strong craving...'Oh that we had meat to eat! We remember the fish we ate in Egypt that cost nothing...but now our strength is dried up, and there is nothing at all but this manna to look at.'"[8]

So God gave them meat. Lots and lots of meat. "Therefore the LORD will give you meat, and you shall eat. You shall not eat just one day, or two days, or five days, or ten days, or twenty days, but a whole month, until it comes out at your nostrils and becomes loathsome to you, because you have rejected the LORD who is among you."[9]

Was God just being spiteful? After all, He had led them into the wilderness for two years, and all they had to eat was manna. Sure, manna was great, but every day, day after day, the same thing over and over again? I'm sure Israel asked the same question, and Moses had an answer ready for them:

> God has led you...in the wilderness, that He might humble

you, testing you to know what was in your heart, whether you would keep His commandments or not. And He humbled you and let you hunger…that…you [may] know that man does not live by bread alone, but…by every word that comes from the mouth of the Lord.[10]

Israel's hunger seems to have led them, not to every word that comes from the mouth of God, but to a desire for Egypt, the very place of bondage God had just delivered them from. But I think their cravings were for more than meat. I think they wanted to leave behind the hard task of following God and to return to the known comfort of slavery. That happens sometimes, doesn't it? The security of bondage can often seem easier than the anxiety of freedom.

Before we think God was unfair for testing Israel the way He did, we should recognize that He put His Son through the same kind of testing. Jesus spent 40 days in the wilderness. And He hungered as they did, fasting for the entire 40 days, His body probably ending up much like Yun's. But when Satan came to tempt Him and appealed to His hunger, telling Him to "command this stone to become bread," Jesus answered him by quoting Moses' answer to Israel's questions: "It is written, 'Man shall not live by bread alone.'"[11]

I think Jesus was telling Satan and Israel and us something very important about our cravings. In our cravings, God means to test our hearts, to see whether we will depend on Him the way Jesus did, and to see whether we will hunger for bread or sex or significance or religion, or if we will hunger for God's words. Our hunger pangs become a test of sorts, showing us what we want most when we feel worst, revealing what we think will satisfy us.

This thought of hungering reminded me of one of the Beatitudes. I have always been puzzled by some of these sayings because some of them seem to have been said just for the sake of metaphor. For example, when Jesus said, "Blessed are those who hunger and thirst for righteousness, for they shall be satisfied," I always thought it was just a nice word picture.[12]

But perhaps He meant what He said.

The apostle John gives us some clues about this kind of hungering and thirsting. In John's Gospel, Jesus said, "Do not labor for the food that perishes, but for the food that endures to eternal life, which the Son of Man will give to you."[13] Interestingly, He said this in Capernaum to some of the crowd of 5000 whom He had miraculously fed the day before with nothing more than five loaves and two fish. In response, the crowd started asking Him for a sign—um, remember yesterday?—and brought up the whole "manna from heaven" thing their forefathers had miraculously received while wandering in the wilderness. The hunger pangs of this crowd revealed what they believed would satisfy them. They wanted food that perishes, not the kind that endures to eternal life.

But Jesus was smart. He saw past their stomach-level desires and focused on their spiritual needs. "It was not Moses who gave you the bread from heaven, but my Father gives you the true bread from heaven…I am the bread of life."[14] The crowd feigned interest in Jesus' bread, asking Him to give it to them. But Jesus went back to the health of their spirits.

He told them, "Whoever comes to me shall not hunger, and whoever believes in me shall never thirst." Drawing on their request for a sign, He went on to say, "Your fathers ate the manna in the wilderness, and they died…[but] I am the living bread that came down from heaven. If anyone eats of this bread, he will live forever. And the bread that I will give for the life of the world is my flesh."[15]

He was on a roll with this bread metaphor, but the ending is a little jarring. "Unless you eat the flesh of the Son of Man and drink His blood, you have no life in you. Whoever feeds on my flesh and drinks my blood has eternal life...for my flesh is true food, and my blood is true drink."[16]

Whoa there! Did He really just say that? And did He really mean it? John later tells us some of His disciples called these "hard sayings," and many of them turned away from Jesus and stopped following Him. I can see why—these *are* hard sayings.

Before we turn away as well, I suppose we should hear Jesus out. "Whoever feeds on my flesh and drinks my blood abides in me, and I in him."[17] He started out by talking about their hunger, using the bread their stomachs desired to show them the Bread their spirits needed. But then He explained what it means to hunger after righteousness. It means hungering after the flesh and blood of Jesus, taking Him in spiritually in the same way we take bread in physically. When we do so, our hunger is satisfied as we abide in Him.

This sounds like something we've heard before.

You probably remember another one of Jesus' metaphors we've already discussed: the vine and the branches. Later in John's Gospel, Jesus says, "I am the vine; you are the branches. Whoever abides in me and I in him, he it is that bears much fruit...if you keep my commandments, you will abide in my love."[18] We can begin to see a connection between feeding on Jesus' flesh and keeping His commandments, between drinking His blood and abiding in Him.

At this point, I don't know if all of this makes you happy or confused or bored, but Jesus meant for it to make you happy. "These things I have spoken to you, that my joy may be in you, and that your joy may be full."[19]

This is the connection back to the beatitude about hungering after righteous-ness, and to the bondage of Egypt Israel longed for instead of the freedom of following God. It helps us understand why Jesus, in drilling the blind

Pharisees for their filthiness, may have chosen the cup as a metaphor for their lives, and why God is the only one who can open our blind eyes to see the true state of spiritual health.

I wonder if the story of the Exodus was more than a story of God's deliverance of His people *from* bondage. That would be like God emptying our cups of those things that hold us in bondage as well, but our cups would still be empty. I think the story of the Exodus was also a story of deliverance *to* blessing, to a "good and broad land, a land flowing with milk and honey."[20] God means to not only empty our cups but also to fill them with blessing. After all, Jesus told His disciples that He said what He said so their joy would be full. When we abide in His love, hungering with childlike faith and simple obedience, He fills our cups to the brim with joy.

If we want our cups to be filled with joy, maybe we need to start by examining our hunger pangs. When God gives us manna, and we hunger for meat, we're choosing slavery over freedom. Or to put it more practically, when God gives us Jesus, and we hunger for food, sex, significance, or religion, we're choosing to have empty, filthy cups rather than full, clean ones. In Romans 6, Paul tells us we are either slaves to sin or slaves to righteousness, and being a slave to righteousness leads to eternal life. So when God removes the chains of sin from our hands and feet, and we begin to fast from the fillings of this world, a deeper kind of hunger will growl within us, a craving for the spiritual filling of righteousness.

Which is Jesus.

To observe our spiritual health, we start with Jesus. God is the one who opens our eyes; otherwise, we may be withered beyond recognition (like Yun) but not know it (like Cal). Cleaning out our cups also starts with Jesus. We can scrub all we like or paint over the mold as many times as we can, but nothing cleans quite like the righteousness of Jesus. And the filling of our cups with blessing starts with Jesus too. Our hunger will lead us to something else or to Him, to a place of loathing or to the fullness of joy.

It's all about Jesus. My ridiculously skinny spirit could use so much more of Him. I think Jesus would give me vitality and life again, maybe so much so that I could be spiritually ripped and maybe even smell a little like sawdust.

I would love to give you a formula for getting more of Jesus in this way, but if there is one, I don't know it myself. Maybe we should just start by figuring out whether we are blind, and what we hunger for, and what we're filling our cups with. If our hunger is for the things of this world, we're not going to be filled with more of Jesus. And even if our cravings are for all the blessings of heaven apart from Jesus, they won't fill us with more of Him.

But if our cravings are for Jesus, and our souls hunger to know Him, to be known by Him, and to treasure Him above all else, I think we'll find our satisfaction. Unlike my first meal after CST, when my hunger was satisfied with the smallest amount of food, Jesus will increase our appetites for more of Him, and He will continue to satisfy them. And all of the things we've wrestled with about love and abiding and childlike faith and simple obedience will develop from that growing place of satisfaction. Maybe then the nice word pictures will take real form, and we can actually believe and say with confidence, "Blessed are those who hunger and thirst for righteousness, for they shall be satisfied."

13. Suffering:

How God Gives Gifts Sometimes

I really love gifts, especially ones that hover.

I don't know if you've ever received a gift that hovers. I hadn't until recently. I usually give normal kinds of gifts, like clothes or jewelry or gift cards. And I get the same kinds of gifts in return, except for the jewelry. But the best gift I have been given was an amazing little remote control helicopter called an Air Hog. It is made of plastic and Styrofoam, so it's not very expensive. But incredibly, it flies much like a regular helicopter. I can make it hover, fly around the room, and (with a fair bit of practice) land on my wife's head.

Anna gave me the Air Hog, and I'm forever grateful to her for it, but I suppose it shouldn't be in the category of "best gifts ever," particularly if I'm thinking about God and trying to figure out how to want more of Him. It should go without saying that the gift of Jesus is the best gift we could ever imagine. The other gifts, like family, friends, a house, food, health, and so forth are all good gifts from God, things we don't deserve but that He's pleased to give to us. But God gave me one more gift recently, something I didn't ask for but He evidently thought I needed.

His gift was a sickness.

This is not a normal gift, and as much as it's in your control, it's not some-thing I'd recommend you give to anyone. God didn't give it to me on my birthday or Christmas; I opened it up one afternoon while in San Jose for work. This particular gift was a nasty sore throat. I'll spare you the details, but it didn't look good. I try to go to the doctor once every five years if possible, but my throat looked pretty bad, so I called around the city to see if I could find anyone to see me. Striking out, I decided I had to go somewhere, so I drove to the ER.

When I arrived, I found a packed house. The waiting room was already full of people even though it was only early afternoon. One man had a bandage on his head; another limped around on what appeared to be a broken ankle. One woman sat in a wheelchair, fast asleep and looking like she might fall out of her chair at any moment. I signed in, was told the wait might be a couple of hours, and took my seat across from this woman, prepared to dive in and catch her if she fell.

I pulled out my Bible and a book and started reading. After two hours, I was called to the next station, where an attendant collected more per-sonal information and told me again the wait might be a couple of hours. I took my seat once more and resumed my reading. Another hour went by, then another. I went back to one of the stations and asked if they knew how long it might be before I would be seen. I was told it would be a couple of hours. It was well into evening at that point, and I soon realized I might be there all night. I looked around at the rest of the room, now full to the brim with hurting and injured people who might be there all night as well.

That was when my internal pager began beeping. I tried to ignore it as I so often do, but as I have already described, it is extremely difficult to turn off. The call was from the Spirit, and God was asking me to get up from my chair, walk over to the far side of the room, and ask if anyone was interested in talking about God or the Bible or Jesus.

I had no interest in doing this, and I told God so outright. Apparently, He was still interested in my obedience because the beeping continued. I came up with an excuse: These people were here because they were injured and wouldn't want to be bothered by some Bible-wielding guy with a sore throat. But God seemed to think they might want to be bothered. I came up with another excuse: If someone was really interested or had a question about God, they could plainly see I was reading a Bible, and they could ask me. Evidently, God preferred the proactive approach that night.

Slowly and steadily the beeping continued, bringing me to a point of decision. The Spirit finally asked me, *Are you willing to do what I am asking you to do?*

I went back and forth for several minutes until I decided that yes, I was willing, although it was an extremely reluctant yes. So there I sat, ready to go and do this thing that would probably make me terribly uncomfortable. But I didn't move. I tried to talk myself into it again, but it didn't work. I was stuck to my seat. I bowed my head to pray, but actually I did this only to delay doing what I had already reluctantly agreed to do.

Finally, filled with what I perceived to be courage from God in the midst of my fear, I grasped my Bible, stood up, walked around the sleeping woman still slumped on the edge of her wheelchair (making sure not to bump into her in the slightest way lest she fall right out of that seat), and approached the far side of the room. As I arrived, I paused momentarily, gazing at all of the people sitting quietly in their seats or on the floor, and I let the tension of the moment build slightly. I started to open my mouth, but no words came out, and I started walking again—straight into the bathroom.

Have you ever gone into a bathroom at a party or a dinner only because you were feeling awkward and didn't know what else to do? I have, and that is exactly why I found myself in front of the sink. I washed my hands, not because they were dirty, but because I had to do something to justify being there.

After I dried my hands, I looked at myself in the mirror, breathed in deeply, prayed a short prayer for courage, and turned to exit the room. I opened the door into a hallway strewn with people sitting against the walls in both directions. I didn't pause this time.

"Hi," I said, realizing I was off to a great start when I saw all eyes lift to see who was breaking the silence. "I've been over there reading my Bible, and since we're all sitting here for what looks to be a long time, I wanted to see if anyone had any thoughts or questions about the Bible or God or Jesus. Maybe something you've always wanted to know but never gotten a good answer to."

Everyone stared at me, and nobody said a word. I think a faucet dripped, or a cricket chirped, or a pin dropped, or something like that. My mind began racing. *Did no one hear me? Maybe I should ask again. Or maybe I should go back and wash my hands once more.*

Finally, a woman down the hall said, "Do you think God can make this line go any faster?" Everyone laughed. *That's right,* I thought, *ha ha ha—real funny.* A man in front of me chimed in: "I think we all just want to see a doctor and that's all."

This was embarrassing. I had done what God asked me to do, and it wasn't working out as I had imagined it would. In my head, everyone within earshot was supposed to gather at my feet in hopeful anticipation, hearts ready to respond to the altar call I would give at the end of my gospel presentation.

People were at my feet, but that was because they were already sitting on the floor. No one gathered.

There was, however, plenty of awkward silence. And a lot of staring. Finally, a young man with long hair and a beard looked up at me and said, "Jesus is the way, the truth, and the life, man." I said, "Right on, bro" and sat down to continue what seemed to be a promising conversation. But our exchange didn't work out as I imagined it would. He told me he was there because of a spider bite on his rear, and it was the second time it had happened, and he couldn't figure out why the spiders were so fond of the inside of his shorts. He said he missed his soul mate, and when I asked what happened to her, he said he hadn't met her yet. He said *man* a lot. The conversation wasn't heading much of anywhere, and it soon ended without an altar call.

I said my pleasantries in parting as I stood to go, and I decided I'd give this whole question thing one more shot. So I went to another part of the room where I repeated my invitation to talk. All of those people stared at me as well, a cricket chirped...you know the drill. One woman kind of smiled at me, and I took that as a sign she might be interested in talking. So I asked her again, but she giggled and said no.

This also was embarrassing. I had persisted in obedience even after a rough start, and I reasoned that God owed me this time. Surely, someone in the ER would be brought to a saving knowledge of Jesus. But no—just more awkward silence.

Finally, a young woman a couple of rows away finally yelled out, "I have a question." *Thank you! I don't know who you are and don't care if you don't want to hear about the gospel. I'm just glad I don't have to stand here anymore looking at these people staring at me.* So I ran over to her, introduced myself, and asked her what her question was.

What transpired was a beautiful beginning to the gospel. She asked me what the Bible said about sinners going to heaven. I told her lots of sinners went to heaven. Having no sin wasn't the point; the point was whether or not you have Jesus, or Jesus has you. She told me she knew very little about the Bible but wanted to know more about God. So I began to tell her the redemptive story of the Bible and its star, Jesus.

The conversation flowed well; she asked great questions, and God provided me with sufficient answers. Her little eight-year-old cousin even asked if she could sit with us and listen. But this beautiful beginning came to a sudden stop. She said her illness made it hard to concentrate, but she really wanted to hear, and would I wait for about two minutes until she came back? I nodded my head and started asking her cousin how old she was and where she went to school and all the other questions you might ask a child.

A few minutes later, the woman returned and said she really wanted to hear more but just couldn't concentrate on having a conversation. I didn't want to press the matter on her, so I smiled and said, "It was great talking to you." As she walked away, I sat there feeling as if a bird had just snatched away the gospel seed from the path.[1] I saw her later on that evening, carrying on a conversation with the spider-bite guy of all people, and I wondered why she had seemed so receptive at first and why she had eventually closed her heart to my words.

To be honest with you, I was bummed. Not so much because her eyes weren't opened to the truth but because there was no payoff for me. I had done something hard for God, and I'd faced ridicule, and I'd pressed on and had the joy of sharing the gospel with someone, and it didn't go anywhere. As I mentioned before, I felt as if God owed me.

So I went back to my seat, discouraged in my spirit but also ticked off that I had been sitting in that room for six hours without seeing a doctor. As I grumbled, another young woman came and sat in the open seat next to me. My internal pager beeped once more, and I looked outside for a nearby lake to throw it into. This time, the Spirit asked me to strike up a conversation with this woman but not use my "Who wants to talk about Jesus?" thing.

But I just sat there. For more than half an hour, I held a conference call with the Spirit over the merits of striking up a conversation with the young woman. I had already obeyed God once, and nothing significant came of it, so I didn't think anything significant would come of another conversation. The Spirit encouraged me to have a little faith.[2]

I was already embarrassed by standing up and asking all those people my questions, and now I just wanted to blend into the crowd. The Spirit reminded me of Jesus' promise that He would be with me always.[3]

I was also sick and tired, literally, of waiting to see a doctor and frankly didn't care anymore. The Spirit reminded me of Paul's tireless ministry for the sake of Jesus and the gospel.[4]

As I fought with God, I tried to distract myself by reading. I happened upon a story of a Masai warrior from Kenya named Joseph who got saved after meeting someone on a road outside his village, went back to his village to share the good news, and got the stuffing beat out of him. In fact, he was beaten so badly that he was dragged by the villagers out into the bush and left for dead. He woke up three days later, covered in cuts and bruises, but he decided to go back into the village to share the gospel once more. Again, he was beaten senseless, left for dead, and woke up days later. But his joy in Christ and his love for his village compelled him to go back. This third time, he was again beaten for perhaps the last time, and as he passed out from the pain, he saw the villagers begin to weep. When he awoke, he was in his own bed, being nursed back to health by the villagers who had nearly beaten him to death. The village had come to Christ.[5]

Joseph the Masai demonstrated the worth and value of the gospel and of Jesus, his prized possessions, things for which he was willing to suffer. And his village came to see God's glory because Joseph valued God's glory more than his own life. As I thought of him, beaten and left for dead, getting up time and time again to go back and do what God had called him to do, I was sickened by my hesitation. Joseph faced barbed wire and fists; I had faced only a stinging word or two. Feeling ashamed, I thought better of my disobedience.

So I turned to this woman seated next to me and asked, "What brought you to the ER?" We spent the next two hours walking through her story: She was 20 years old and had two kids out of wedlock and had abused drugs and alcohol for the past three years. She had also tried to kill herself three months before that time, and she was in the ER to treat ovarian cysts. She confided to me that she used to go to church but hadn't been since the birth of her firstborn because she was too ashamed of what she had done. But by the end of our conversation, she had reaffirmed her faith in Jesus and committed to start reading her Bible again. She also made plans to attend church that weekend for the first time in years.

This was a good ending, and it was a good payoff. But it should have been a good story and a good payoff even if nothing else had happened that night. The point of the night for me wasn't about the good that comes from evangelism. I think God may sometimes ask us to stand up in public and ask, "Who wants to talk about Jesus?" and at other times He may just ask us to start a normal conversation with someone. I think the point of the night had to do with the gift He had given me, the gift of sickness and a trip to the ER and all the good that comes from suffering.

Jesus said, "Blessed are you when others revile you and persecute you and utter all kinds of evil against you falsely on my account. Rejoice and be glad, for your reward is great in heaven."[6] This is not something I can immediately grasp. I had faced persecution that night, although in a very small way, and I didn't feel blessed. I felt angry, embarrassed, ashamed, tired, sick, and guilty, but I didn't feel blessed.

I know the Christian life is filled with paradox, but I wondered if this was taking it a little too far. Should I call my sore throat a gift from God? Wouldn't it make more sense to say I got a sore throat for no reason at all, and God simply took my sore throat and then made some good out of it?

I went back to Scripture and started reading all the verses I could find on suffering. This was not a fun exercise. I found passage after passage that kept linking the Christian life to suffering, and as I looked at my own life and how very little I had suffered, I began to wonder what I might be missing. I wonder how you might react to some of the Scriptures, what you would think when you read them, whether you'd be confused by them or be angry at them or find some sort of hope in them.

Here are a few comments from Jesus: "You will be hated by all for my name's sake." "Whoever does not take his cross and follow me is not worthy of me." "If they persecuted me, they will also persecute you."[7]

If those weren't enough, here are a couple from Peter: "If when you do good and suffer for it you endure, this is a gracious thing in the sight of God. For to this you have been called." "Since therefore Christ suffered in the flesh, arm yourselves with the same way of thinking."[8]

Or Paul, no stranger to suffering: "All who desire to live a godly life in Christ Jesus will be persecuted." "Through many tribulations we must enter the kingdom of God." "For it has been granted to you that for the sake of Christ you should not only believe in him but also suffer for his sake."[9]

All of these statements are tough to deal with, but the last statement is the one that blows my mind. How can Paul, the same Paul who was lashed, beaten with rods, stoned, shipwrecked, imprisoned, hungry, cold, and in constant toil and hardship, say, "It has been granted to you...[to] suffer"? Did he really just call suffering a gift?

If suffering is a gift, I guess I can understand why Jesus calls us blessed when we are persecuted, why Peter tells us to rejoice in suffering, and why James tells us to consider our trials as cause for joy.[10] After all, gifts are blessings. I like gifts, especially ones that hover, but I suppose this means I should also like gifts like sore throats, even if they are a very small kind of suffering.

But that's the issue: How do I go about learning to rejoice in suffering? Enjoying a flying helicopter or a new surfboard is easy, but receiving a sickness or ridicule with joy is much more difficult. I know my ridiculously skinny spirit needs more of Jesus, and I know He was "a man of sorrows, and acquainted with grief," so maybe I can learn from Him how to rejoice in suffering.[11]

I would expect the Bible to make much of Jesus' suffering, to make a show of how much pain He endured on our behalf. If I were Jesus, and my Spirit were inspiring the writing of the Gospels, I'd make sure everyone knew I suffered more than anyone else ever had, that I had suffered the most and nothing could add to what I had gone through.

But Paul wrote, "Now I rejoice in my sufferings for your sake, and in my flesh I am filling up what is lacking in Christ's afflictions for the sake of His body, that is, the church."[12] *Filling up what is lacking in Christ's afflictions?* What on earth is Paul talking about? How could Jesus be lacking in anything? Jesus certainly suffered while He was here on earth. For three years, He was in ministry and faced homelessness, harsh living conditions, instability, unbelief, taunts, rejection, slander, a constant onslaught of people in need, sleepless nights, extended periods of fasting and temptation, and death threats. And His betrayal, arrest, false trial, beatings, crucifixion, and broken union with the Father at the climax of the cross brought pain and suffering we can't even imagine.

Yet in spite of all the hardship Jesus suffered in His life, Paul seemed to believe something was still lacking in His afflictions. And Paul was intent on filling up what was lacking for the sake of Christ's body, the church.

I didn't know what to make of all this, so I began to pray about it. Feeling somewhat ashamed that my life has been virtually pain free (except in CST), and knowing I've experienced very little hardship, I began to ask God how I might be able to fill up the remainder of Christ's afflictions. I don't think I actually prayed for suffering, but I think I came close.

God answered that prayer in His own way, in His own time, and in very small steps for me. I began to encounter minor trials of every kind: physical, emotional, and spiritual. I had hurt my legs while running the LA Marathon a few years earlier, and they started hurting once more. I went to rehab for months but could never fix the problem. A few weeks later, I went through a difficult period in my Christian community, facing the darkness of my own heart as well as persecution from other believers. I won't go into the details, but the going was tough for a while. And a few weeks after that, I was diagnosed with an iron overload disorder, a sickness that required me to give a pint of blood every week for several months straight.

All of these struggles, as small as they may have been, came in regular succession. A time of trial would come, and I would wrestle with it, praying about it and trying to figure out God's purpose in it all. After a while, I'd feel a sense of peace from God about whatever was going on, somewhat confident that I had endured my trial and learned what I needed to know about suffering. But then something else would come up, and I'd go through the same cycle all over again. Only after the third or fourth time did the thought occur to me that my life might always include some form of suffering.

You may have lost a parent or a child, been diagnosed with cancer, or been abused at some point in your life, and you might take exception with my use of the word *suffering* to describe my insignificant troubles. I don't blame you one bit. I just invite you to consider with me how your own suffering may be filling up what is lacking in Christ's afflictions.

This idea didn't make much sense at first, but I'm beginning to see why Paul was honored to partner with Jesus in filling up what remains of His afflictions. Paul seemed to believe that God wanted Christ and His body, the church, to suffer for the sake of the gospel, and that through an appointed measure of suffering, God will reach the world with the good news that Jesus is worth every moment of hardship. Suffering for His sake seems to show that He is to be valued more than freedom from discomfort, that living by faith in the promise of eternity with God is worth far more than any cost in this world.

If we hear this and think of God as a merciless tyrant who finds pleasure in the pain of others, I bet Paul would tell us we've missed the point. He would probably say God is glorified when the world sees that Jesus is the believer's prized possession, that He is the best kind of gift and is worth so much more than any amount of loss, suffering, pain, or persecution.

My friend Billy learned this lesson while flat on his back in sub-Saharan Africa. He went on the same trip to Burkina Faso that Anna and I went on, and while he was there, he came down with malaria. He's a rock-solid man of God, the leader of our group at church, secretly nerdy in an engineering sort of way but immensely popular with the girls at church nonetheless, and a pretty outgoing and funny guy. But this sickness absolutely hammered him, reducing him to a nearly motionless state. After days of dehydration and weakness and pain, Billy wrote this while lying in bed:

> I've learned a greater appreciation for the suffering of Christ on the cross. The pain I feel now is only a fraction of Christ's pain on the cross, and this is profound. Being sick in sub-Saharan Africa really starts to put things in perspective. I realize that the clothes I wear, the car I drive, and the computer I have all matter very little in comparison to this illness. Suffering exposes the trivial for what it is. Just think, people all around the world are sick, just like this, but all I care about is getting a cool-looking cell phone.[13]

Billy's encounter with suffering led him to a place of humility, the same place Job, the poster child for suffering, went when he replied to God, "I have uttered what I did not understand, things too wonderful for me, which I did not know...therefore I despise myself and repent in dust and ashes."[14] But God lifted Job out of his anguish and blessed him, and He did the same for Billy. Billy's last journal entry in Africa included this:

> I've learned there is a reward for suffering.[15] I cannot wait to get to heaven and have God reveal to me what has happened because of my suffering here. What if someone comes to the Lord because of this and I get to see them in heaven? That eternal reward will be sweet indeed, but there are already immediate rewards from the wisdom gained from God and the deepening of my faith. These are far more valuable than any other thing on earth.

It's hard to convey in a few short paragraphs what it's like to watch a guy fight for joy in the midst of illness. But it was inspiring to me. Billy's journal reminded me of the words of Paul: "I count everything as loss because of the surpassing worth of knowing Christ Jesus my Lord. For His sake I have suffered the loss of all things and count them as rubbish, in order that I may gain Christ."[16]

When I said God is glorified when the world sees that Jesus is the believer's prized possession, worth any amount of loss, this is what I was talking about. Billy began to see what Paul knew—the surpassing worth of knowing Christ, the conviction that He is so valuable that everything else in the world is like trash in comparison.

Imagine that—your wonderful family, your beautiful home, the good health you have, those meaningful friends, the wealth God has blessed you with, that perfect job—they're all like garbage. Don't get me wrong; God is a

God of blessing and good gifts, but those things are like trash when we compare them to the greater value of knowing Jesus.

This has been one of the things I've had to wrestle with. What constitutes a good gift? If you had asked me recently what good gifts God has given me, I would have rattled off a list like the one above. And they are good gifts. But a better gift, according to Paul, is to know Jesus. In fact, it's a surpassingly better gift, the kind of gift that fills your cup with joy.

And this is where my theology comes up short. God seems to be saying that suffering is a path to knowing Jesus in an increasingly intimate way. So if suffering takes me closer to the heart of Jesus, and Jesus is the best gift, then suffering must be a good gift too, right?

But this isn't a natural fit for my way of thinking. I am used to thinking of suffering as something negative, something to wrestle through. Sure, we can rely on God in the midst of it, but it's still a bummer. So when I read a verse that says, "For those who love God all things work together for good," I translate that into "all things work together for my happiness or my comfort."[17] I struggle with accepting suffering as part of the "all things" God is working together for my good, even though "all things" must certainly mean *all* things, including suffering.

I wonder if you have the same struggle. Do you view suffering as a gift? Do you know the honor of suffering in order to fill up what is lacking in Christ's afflictions, to show the world Jesus is more valuable than all worldly treasures? Or are you like me, wanting more of God but really wanting more of the good things from God?

If we believe deeply in God's sovereignty, I don't think we have much choice but to trust that He knows better than we do what is best for our lives. If we trust Him but view suffering as a nuisance, we need to go to war with our understanding of good. We need a new definition of good, a renewed confidence that having Jesus is good and that anything that takes us closer to Jesus is good as well.

If this is true, then my sore throat was a gift, and the pain in my legs was a gift, and my persecution at the ER was a gift, and Joseph's beatings were a gift, and all of your own trials, both great and small, have been gifts from God for your good. They are part of His good purposes and will, regardless of whether we recognize and embrace them.[18]

Do you want more of this kind of God? Is this the kind of God you can crave, the kind of God for whom you can hunger and thirst?

We need to keep in mind that He is *good* as we seek to fill up what is lacking in Christ's afflictions so the world will know that Jesus is more valuable to us than gold, or silver, or health, or comfort. I can understand why you might struggle with a God who gives both blessing and suffering as gifts. But we struggle with this because part of us believes that life now is more important than life later. Something in us wants to hold on to our comfort in life rather than our comfort in eternity.

Consider this: Your life is like "a vapor that appears for a little while and then vanishes," so the times of blessing are vapors too, as are the times of trial.[19] Both vanish quickly, so neither should hold much sway over our lives. Believing that our lives are like vapors, that family and Air Hogs and sore throats and persecution are all vapors, allows us to join Paul and Billy in this affirmation:

Nothing, whether great or small, blessing or suffering, compares to knowing Jesus.

14. Joy:

Why God Is
to Be Treasured

Kids with no shoes smile more than kids with shoes.

I know that sounds definitive, as if I know for certain that it's true. I actually haven't conducted a formal study on the topic, so I guess stating my conclusion so directly could be misleading. But I suspect it's true, and I'll explain why in a moment.

But before we get to that, consider how ridiculous my statement seems at first glance. Shoes are great; they are comfortable and fashionable and effective at protecting our feet. Personally, I haven't ever gone without shoes for an extended period of time, and I consider myself a pretty happy person. So why would a kid with no shoes be happier than me?

Presumably, a number of humans walked the face of the earth before shoes were invented. After all, the traditional interpretation of God's response to Adam and Eve's sin was that He fashioned garments from animal skins and clothed their bodies; it says nothing of Him making slippers out of little bunnies. And today, I find myself, a remote descendant of Adam and Eve, wearing shoes. So someone along the line between them and me must have been the first person to wear shoes.

Whoever this pioneer was, he or she must have felt as if this was the world's greatest invention. Imagine yourself spending the better part of your youth walking across hardened soil and rocky paths and hot sand and cold clay, all in bare feet. You would not think much of it because you would have always walked around in bare feet, just like everyone else. In fact, you would not think of feet as being bare at all; you would simply think of them as feet.

But as you slipped into that first pair of fuzzy slippers or cushioned cross-trainers, or even a shard of animal skin with a vine for straps, imagine the smile that would slowly spread across your face.

You would take your new shoes and walk through the mud and find your feet still clean and dry. Or you might venture out through the desert under the height of the sun's gaze without jumping from one foot to the other. Perhaps you would shove a friend and then run into a field with thorny underbrush just to see if he would chase you.

Eventually, you would stop relishing the fact that you were the only person on the planet with a pair of shoes, and you would help your friends or your mother or your cousins make their own pairs of shoes. And as you watched them test out their new feet on the rocky path, you would see smiles spread across their faces. This would make you smile even more.

Soon enough, your entire village would be walking around in shoes, and everyone would be smiling. Fewer people would have cuts on their feet, and more work could be done to make the village a better place in which to live. The world would open up to you just a bit more, and perhaps you would take a long trip to a village you had never visited before. You and your happy friends would embark, striding confidently and comfortably along your path regardless of what lay beneath your feet.

Eventually, you would come to a village, and you would walk to the center of all the huts, and you would notice that the people, although friendly and welcoming, were not smiling as much as you and your friends were. This would make all the sense in the world to you because they did not have shoes. While you were there, you might show them how to make shoes, and you would see them smile, and this would cause you to smile even more. And the fact that you were continuing to smile more and more would make you smile still more; the joy in smiling would perpetuate itself.

Near the end of your life, as you looked back on all you had accomplished, you might even consider the experience of inventing shoes to be your greatest achievement. You would think of the hundreds or thousands of people who had improved the quality of their lives because of your discovery. And as you breathed your last few breaths, an enormous grin would spread across your face, revealing the happiness that came to your life through shoes.

So when I say that kids with no shoes smile more than kids with shoes, it's clear that history, at least my version of history, would tell us otherwise. But I still think it may be true.

I'll tell you why. When my friends and I were in Burkina Faso, we traveled each day from the capital city, Ouagadougou, to a rural village called Saonre where the orphan center was located. When we arrived at the center on the first day, we found scores of little children, some of whom had torn clothing and most of whom were without shoes.

As we slowly climbed out of our vans, these children gathered around us in a semicircle, staring at us quietly, lips drawn tightly into stoic poses. We looked back at them, not knowing exactly what to do or say. A moment of awkwardness hung in the air. But then someone in our group waved to them and smiled. And a hundred little teeth shone back brightly in the morning sun.

I have never seen kids smile so big. Or so much.

Joy oozed out of these kids; everything in them delighted to look at us, to smile at us, to touch us, and to laugh uncontrollably at us as we tried to speak their language. They carried our bags, smiling the entire way. They held our hands and walked around the grounds, grinning from ear to ear. All we had to do was look directly at them, and they would break out with joy.

Throughout the workday, as we were slaving over shovels beneath the hot African sun, we would look over at eight-year-old boys or ten-year-old girls pushing wheelbarrows full of dirt. And they were smiling.

Mind you, they didn't have any shoes. They also didn't have parents. Or a change of clothing, or a bed to sleep in, or much food. But they were still smiling.

One of the boys I connected with on the trip is named Mardoche. One morning, as I was mixing cement for the local builders, Mardoche came up to me and made a sign to follow him. So I laid my shovel on the ground and followed him across the grounds. He stopped at the edge of one of the buildings and looked around the corner, and then he beckoned me to come along quietly.

He was being very secretive, so naturally I thought we were going to do something that wasn't allowed, which is always a good time. But as we came to the back of the building, Mardoche looked over his shoulder once more and then put his two hands up to me. In each grubby hand was a piece of bread, one of the two food items he was given to eat each day. He took a bite out of one of the pieces of bread and handed me the other. As I slowly took it from his hand, he looked up at me and said, "Fo ya mum soa," which means, "You are my friend."

I took a bite, looking down at this little boy with no money, no iPod, no Xbox, no suit, no Legos, no soccer balls, no college savings account, no change of clothes, no parents, and no shoes. Just a ragged T-shirt, a pair of shorts, two little loaves, and the biggest grin this side of heaven.

Mardoche is how I know that kids without shoes smile more than kids with shoes. When I got home from CST, I never considered giving half my food to someone else. I might have given them a bite, but not a big bite, and I probably would have secretly resented them a little. Even if I were overcome with charity and did give half of my food to someone else, I definitely would not smile uncontrollably.

I am still a fan of shoes though. I don't think giving up shoes is necessarily the path to knowing the joy of the Lord. But something about Mardoche's kind of joy is different from my own; he seems to have more of it. All of the kids were like him—so joyful, so giving, yet with hardly anything to call their own.

Jesus talked a lot about joy. So did Paul. And Peter and John and David and Isaiah and Habakkuk and Solomon and James and Jeremiah and whoever wrote 1 Kings. Which ultimately means that God talked a lot about joy. He seems completely intent on us having this joy. We might even say He created us for joy. Or joy for us. Or maybe both.

The Bible speaks about joy in a variety of ways, some of which we might expect and others that don't seem to make sense. We can find joy in good news. We can also find joy as a result of great suffering. We can even find joy by hearing good news *while* suffering.[1]

We also find other spiritual realities or emotions that open the door to this kind of joy. Our salvation produces great joy because we know what we have been saved from and where God means to bring us. Peter says the joy that comes in salvation is "inexpressible and filled with glory." Even sorrow and mourning ultimately lead to unfailing joy.[2]

John wrote his Gospel and the truth about fellowship with God and Jesus so that our joy may be complete. Paul said his joy would be made complete when believers are of the same mind with one another. James even tells us to "count it joy" when we face trials and suffering.[3]

But God has not limited this joy to just humanity. Even the earth is supposed to get in on all this action. When Solomon was anointed king over Israel, "all the people went up after him…rejoicing with great joy, so that the earth was split by their noise." David tells all of creation to "shout for joy to God." The heavens sparkle with good cheer, the seas roar with delight, the fields roll with laughter, and the trees of the forest break forth in song, swinging to the melody of their praises and clapping their hands before their Maker.[4]

We can find joy in good and bad times. It can help us not only endure life but even make life worth living. We are to count our trials as joy, seek joy, make joy complete, and make joy full. Joy exists to make our priorities clear to us. It speaks to us loudly when we taste and see how satisfying it is and softly when we ignore its superior quality. When we experience God's kind of joy, we know we want it above all else, but we're not sure how to go about getting it.

I hope this has convinced you God thinks a lot about joy. But I think we should also wonder why He does so.

Joy seems to be a more spiritual term than *happiness,* but *happiness* is a good proxy for *joy* and makes it a little easier to understand. When I say everyone wants to be happy, you know what I mean. You want to be happy. I want to be happy. Even grumpy people who give us the finger on the highway or yell at the toaster want to be happy, although they don't show it very well.

I pursue happiness all the time. In fact, it might be my most important priority. I make nearly all my decisions with my own personal happiness in mind. When I get up in the morning to have breakfast, I think about whether the chocolate chip oatmeal cookies would make me happier than the grapes and the cereal that tastes like bark. When a friend e-mails a bunch of us to ask for help moving on Saturday, I consider whether that (and the pizza he offers for lunch) would make me happier than surfing all morning and then eating four waffles.

Everyone I know appears to pursue happiness all the time as well. My wife finds a ridiculous amount of happiness in colorful shoes. My parents found a great deal of happiness living in Kauai for nine years, though I can't possibly imagine how they did so. Some of my friends seem to find happiness driving a specific kind of car. Others find it watching football. Some guys I know from work would swear they find happiness by hitting the bars and looking for girls.

All this makes sense to me, that we all pursue our own happiness and chase after joy, because we're self-interested people and because we're products of our environment. And our culture tells us that happiness is *the* goal to be sought after and bought. Aren't commercials claiming to sell us happiness when they show us a pretty girl smiling at a guy who has just popped a new kind of gum? And when men buy that new kind of gum instead of the one in the plain wrapper, do they not somehow think they are buying a small piece of that happiness? We don't buy it for the sake of the pretty girl; we buy it for our own sake, so the pretty girl will like us and perhaps come close to us.

As selfish as we are today, this isn't a modern phenomenon. Our founding fathers considered happiness an "unalienable right" for all free men and women. They were willing to start a revolution, go to war, lose their own lives or the lives of their families, live in exile from their native land, and labor beneath the burden of leading a new nation, all to preserve their right to live freely and happily. And to top it all off, the United States

Supreme Court has also weighed in on the issue of happiness. In an 1884 case called *Butchers' Union Co. v. Crescent City Co.,* Justice Samuel Miller wrote this:

> Among those unalienable rights, as proclaimed in [the Declaration of Independence], is the right of men to pursue their happiness...so as to give to them their highest enjoyment.

I'm sure Justice Miller was a very smart and nice man, but my question for him would be this: If our highest enjoyment comes from gaining wealth or knowledge, why was Mardoche so happy when he gave me half his food?

After all, giving me half of his food cost Mardoche something—half of his food, to be precise. I have to assume he would have enjoyed eating his own food, because he doesn't get much of it in the first place. Yet he made a very clear choice that came from his own desire for happiness, and that choice was to give me what he himself could have enjoyed. He evidently weighed his options—either he could eat his food and be happy, or he could give some of it to me and be even happier—and he chose his own greatest joy.

If you're like me, you might think choosing our greatest joy is selfish in the same way that pursuing our own happiness each day can seem selfish. But Mardoche demonstrated otherwise, and John Piper has helped me to see that God means for us to maximize our joy by choosing that which will bring us our greatest pleasure: Him.[5]

Our craving for happiness and joy is from God. He created us with a craving that longs to be filled. And when we fill this hole with anything but Him, we realize none of it works. We find ourselves in a story that has been told for centuries. As the pages turn in our lives, each chapter brings a new pursuit that eventually ends in disappointment. The plot twists and turns, but the cast of characters remains the same: security, comfort, wealth, power, sex, success, popularity, status…anything and everything we believe will bring us fulfillment. We fail to read between the lines, to see the beauty of the story behind the story. I think we misunderstand the point of the craving itself.

Joy or happiness is what we all crave, but we can satisfy it in only one way. We cannot make joy our ultimate aim because we are not pure enough to seek after it in the right way. We must seek to satisfy our longings, the deepest cravings of our soul, by seeking the One who made us with a desire for Him.

This is the purpose of our cravings. They are signs that lead us to Him.

Before John the Baptist tasted air for the first time, he knew joy came from being close to Jesus.[6] Paul recognized that joy comes as a fruit of being intimately united with the Spirit.[7] David found an excess of joy in the presence of the Father.[8] He also knew that the fullness of joy lay only in the presence of his God.[9]

Many wise men and women have found this joy in being close to Jesus, and they know it is something worth more than the earth's best treasures. Many stories tell us about God's kind of joy and why He is worthy of sacrifice. One old story about such joy bears retelling here.

Once a man was walking along the road outside his town, coming back from a trip to another town on business. This man had his life together: a good wife whom he loved, two small children who were the delight of his eye, a growing and successful local business, and a new home he had built for his family. Life wasn't perfect for this man, but it sure was pretty good.

This man had traveled most of the day, and as he walked, he found himself daydreaming about his life, contemplating his future for himself and his family. He was beginning to find significance in his life, and he was grateful for all the things he had. The wind picked up slightly, blowing a cloud of dust across his path and bringing him back from his musings. He looked around him, realizing he had wandered just off the main road onto the edge of a field on the outer limits of his town.

As the sun dropped closer toward dusk, the man turned back toward the road, but as he neared the edge of the field, his foot caught something in the dirt. He tripped, catching himself with his hand before he fell. As he regained his footing, he turned to see what had caused him to stumble.

Sticking out of one of the plow lines was a gnarled piece of wood. He pulled away some of the topsoil, revealing a hint of metal. He took a knee and dug some more. Soon, the side of a small box emerged, and as the last rays of light cast about the field, he finally pulled the box from the soil. Night had come, but just enough light remained for the man to put his fingers to the latch. When it opened, he leaned in closely, finding himself staring at hundreds of gold coins. He picked one up, turning it over in his hand while turning over his future in his head. This was no small find; this box contained enough gold to provide for his family for the rest of his life.

The man jumped to his feet and looked around anxiously. His mind raced with questions. Why was this box of gold buried in the ground? Could he keep it? Whom did it all belong to? He thought about taking the box home, but it was far too heavy. He considered taking several coins in his pocket, but he realized that might arouse suspicion from his family or any neighbors who found out. So he decided to put the box back where he found it.

When he finally reached his home, he burst through the door completely out of breath. His wife and children jumped to their feet, first alarmed by the sudden commotion but then happy to see him. He hugged his family and then pulled his wife aside to tell her what he had found, describing what he had done and seen in every last detail. She had never seen him so excited.

The next day, the man arose from a night of nervous sleep and went to some of the other men in the town, inquiring as to the owner of the large field just outside of town. Before long, he found the owner and went to his home to meet with him. He offered to buy the field, but the owner set a price that was ten times what a field of that size was normally worth.

The man ran home and again told his wife everything that had happened. She said the price was way too high. But the man knew better; he had seen the gold and knew it to be worth hundreds of times the price of the field. All he had to do was come up with the money. He would have to sell all they owned: their house, their livestock, their furniture, their clothes, and their business.

So that is exactly what he did. Leaving everything behind was agonizing, but the man knew what he had to do. Every last thing he and his family owned was sold off to neighbors and friends. Parting with his clothes and furniture and livestock was easy. The business was much harder. He had invested so much of his identity in it, and he had great dreams for its future, but he finally decided it had to go. His home was the hardest to give up. He and his father had built his home themselves, and it held many good and precious memories. His wife cried quietly as he signed over the deed.

Finally, once everything was gone, the man took the money he had received and went back to the owner of the field. He presented himself, weary from all of the work of the past week but happy nonetheless. Laying the outrageous sum on the owner's table, the man said he had come to buy the field. The owner looked at the money and then at the man.

"Why have you done this?" he asked. "Why have you sold all that you have, everything you have worked for your entire life, to buy this field?"

The man replied to him, "I have traded everything in my life for this field because I know that what I have lost cannot compare to what I will gain."

And Jesus said to His disciples, "The kingdom of heaven is like treasure hidden in a field, which a man found and covered up. Then in his joy he goes and sells all that he has and buys that field."[10]

According to Jesus, joy comes when someone finds something worth giving everything up for. Jesus knew this kind of joy firsthand. He gave everything up for His treasure. He shed His heavenly glory for a time, separated Himself from joy-filled fellowship with His Father, took on human flesh, and submitted to the wrath of God, each decision a part of selling all He had because of the treasure he gained in the process: us.

But this parable isn't about Him treasuring us. It's about us treasuring Him.

Because Jesus is most valuable, I want to be facedown in the dirt, hands digging furiously to uncover something more precious than anything the earth can offer. I don't want to stop at accepting the gospel, or view the things of this world as my primary blessings, or even rest in the promise of heaven as the goal of my faith. I want to give up anything and everything that competes with Jesus for the allegiance of my heart. When John Piper asks, "If you could have heaven, with no sickness, and with all the friends you ever had on earth, and all the food you ever liked, and all the leisure activities you ever enjoyed, and all the natural beauty you ever saw…could you be satisfied…if Christ was not there?"[11] I want to be able to answer with a resounding no.

I suspect the man who bought the field would feel likewise. He didn't want the field for the sake of the field; he wanted it for the treasure that was in the field. And we shouldn't long for the blessings of this life or even heaven for the sake of heaven. We should ache for the Treasure who will be there. Would that my heart would ache with desire for the Treasure I have found, for this desire to consume all my thoughts and drive away all of my other ambitions so I am left with nothing but this one all-consuming pursuit.

Forgive me for waxing poetic. Actually, that sentiment is quite difficult to live out. My heart isn't consumed with this desire; it's filled with a longing for a new job, some extra sleep, an iPhone, or a comfortable life that doesn't require too much of my time to seek after God. But God has given me a small taste of joy at times, just enough for me to know where I can find it.

I'm thinking of a church service I attended at my parents' church in Knoxville. Pastor John taught powerfully from Scripture that morning, and after he finished, the worship pastor led the congregation in one final song. I remember singing that day, truly worshipping God with my mind, heart, and spirit for one of the few times in my life, and for a brief moment I felt as if I had joined an immense multitude of believers praising God in heaven. A shiver went through my entire body, and I found myself smiling uncontrollably, almost laughing. This small taste of joy was incredibly sweet.

You remember Billy, my friend with malaria. Billy once told me a story about seeking the joy to be found in fellowship with God. He said he was in his bedroom one evening, listening to worship songs through his headphones while working on something. He said the words to one of the songs spoke powerfully to his heart, and he felt incredibly moved by them, feeling the great weight of God's presence in his room. He too described a sensation of joy in the immanence of God's presence. The next day, he came home from work, went straight into his room, put his headphones on, cranked up the same song, and waited for the joy once more.

But nothing happened. God did not show up in the same way. Billy was left with the normal feeling of sitting on his bed with his headphones on, which was a little awkward.

Billy's story reminded me of my own, and I realized that joy is meant to be sought after, not for the sake of the experience, but for the sake of being with the One who gives us that joy. And it's not something we can replicate anytime we like. When we try to do so, we turn the experience into an idol and worship it instead of God. Our cravings for more of Him and the joy we find in Him are both gifts, but we should always value the Giver far more than the gift.

We don't always feel God's presence, and we aren't always consumed with this kind of joy we've been talking about. But even in those times, we can remember that we will find the greatest kind of joy in Him and that we do what's best for ourselves when we orient our lives around Jesus, knowing that even if we experience some measure of sorrow in this life, the life to come will bring the fullness of joy in His presence.

I am reminded of the joy of my friends in Africa. Mardoche may not be experiencing joy because he is earnestly seeking God with all of his heart. Perhaps he knows joy because he is unencumbered by the things of this world. After all, he doesn't have to choose between trusting God to provide for him and trusting an ATM to have cash that day, because his only provider is God. But he has great joy nonetheless because of his love for God. He values God more than possessions, and this is the perspective that makes him so generous. It's what makes him so happy too.

I want this kind of joy, and I hope you do as well. What will our lives look like when we value God more than anything else in our lives? If we could have all the treasures of the world, great wisdom, and unrivaled power, or if we could just have a new job or a husband or a wife, or if we could even have the kingdom of heaven all to ourselves, would we count all of it as loss because of the surpassing worth of knowing Jesus? As we yield our grip on our own personal treasures so we can take hold of the ultimate Treasure, we may find God calling us to literally give everything up to follow Him. Or He may ask us to simply let go of everything within our hearts so He can take full control of our lives.

That's when we'll be able to smile like a kid with no shoes.

15. End:

How to Get So Much More of God

That kid with the ice cream needs a bigger spoon.

You will recall the chubby little boy attacking a quart of ice cream with reckless intensity, the one whose heart and soul are singularly focused on how much frozen goodness he can stuff into his face at once. He is consumed by the passion of his desire, ignoring everything else in the world but the feast that is set before him. The only thing limiting this boy from experiencing the greatest joy he could possibly imagine is the size of his spoon.

I started out as a comfortable Christian with a small spoon. I tried everything I could think of to be a better Christian, to shake off my cloak of comfort, to strain with all my might to stretch my spoon into something larger. I tried forming habits but failed to keep them. I developed spiritual disciplines but then lost self-control. I sought to be bold for Jesus but discovered my own pride in the process. I embraced religion and all its virtues but became a legalist along the way. And I found my purpose through simple obedience but resented God in spite of it.

I'm a mess at times, but I've also set my eyes on the greatest joy I can imagine: Jesus. I know I do not always live this way, and I'm hesitant even to try to share with you how to go about finding this kind of joy in Him. I'm grateful you have joined me in this journey, but to tell you the truth, the journey has just begun.

Much of my story to this point has been about me and all of my attempts to crave more of God. I feel as if I have been in a hurry to accomplish things for God, running alone down this path into a headwind. Progress has been slow as I've fought my way through fear and insecurity, uncertain at times about which way to go when I come to a fork in the road. I've had to grit my teeth, do my best, and continue pounding the pavement. And to be honest, I'm tired of doing it alone. If you find yourself exhausted from your own strivings for spirituality, I hope you've found some solidarity with me on this journey.

But the journey ahead seems quite different. The focus seems to be less on us and more on Jesus. We don't have to walk this road alone because Jesus is with us and the Spirit is blowing a gentle tailwind as we walk. We can be in less of a hurry, realizing the journey is as important as the destination because of whom we're traveling with, and we can trust Him to lead us instead of feeling the burden to find our own way. When we gaze ahead, the path appears more difficult in some ways, with deeper valleys and higher peaks, but it also looks to be a road worth traveling, one with much greater rewards.

As we've discussed my different cravings for more of God and all the silly things I've done in pursuit of Him, I've realized what was happening was not so much an addition of something that intensified my cravings for God but rather a stripping away of the things that smothered them. Our cravings for more of Him are already there, and when we don't find them being satisfied, we need to ask ourselves, and more importantly God, why that is so. As He answers our question and uncovers these longings, our focus will return to where it belongs: on God, the Creator and satisfier of our cravings, so that we will make much of God rather than much of ourselves.

Living like this will help us to embrace being an extra so that we're happy when the Star gets all the glory and the credit. We'll be able to hear the Spirit as He pages us, and our response will be one of simple obedience. We'll reconnect with God in childlike faith, taking in the bread of life and being satisfied instead of feeding our hunger with things that won't last. And we'll count everything as loss, from our greatest earthly treasures to our hardest times of suffering, because of the superior value of and joy in knowing Jesus.

As we live out this kind of life that seeks to make much of God, we may find our tendency is to go back to religion, to believe our cravings for God are going to be satisfied by going to church more, or reading more Scripture every day, or praying for longer periods of time, or serving in more ministries. Or we may also find our tendency is to throw all of that out the window, to revel in the freedom of grace that tells us God loves us just the way we are, which means we don't have to do anything at all.

I suspect you know there's a balance to be sought between these extremes. Reading, praying, serving, and any other expressions of craving more of God are useless without our hearts. That's why we need to sing alongside Pastor Robinson, who described the wandering of our hearts in his great hymn and ended with a prayer we need to pray every day. "Prone to wander, Lord, I feel it, / Prone to leave the God I love. / Here's my heart, O, take and seal it, / Seal it for Thy courts above."

Giving our hearts to God is a day by day, month by month, year by year process of growing in intimacy with Him, discovering more about His person and His characteristics, and fully comprehending how much He loves us. When we give Him more of our hearts, we offer Him the best of our hopes and dreams and fears and time and money and talents and love. When we give Him our hearts, we give Him all we are. And when He has our hearts, then our actions, like spiritual disciplines or works of love, will naturally flow from the intimacy we have with Him.

I think the point of our cravings is to be satisfied, not to keep craving. And my experience shows me that knowing and being known by Jesus is the only way we can satisfy them. So I think I can now say Jesus has my heart, or at least I'm giving more and more of it to Him. I'm giving Him my heart because He created me and because He died for my sins and saved me. But most of all, I'm giving Him my heart because He is the most worthy person to receive it.

I told you at the beginning that God is growing within me a longing for joy to be found only in Him. I said this longing is the birth pangs of my cravings, born from the quiet longings of my heart, sounding to the deepest point of my soul. And I wanted so much more of what I was finding there.

What I found deep within me was God. As I shed all of the external layers of religion and sorted through the sins that lay deep inside me, I eventually found Him beneath it all. He was there, waiting to give me a bigger spoon, ready to give me more of Himself as I gave Him more of myself. He was the source of my cravings, sending them up through my soul and into my body, because He knew they would lead me on a search for satisfaction that would point me back to the joy of being with Him.

My desire is that you also find Him in the depths of your soul, speaking to you through your cravings. And many years from now, I hope you will still be there with Him, laughing with joy and loving Him with all your heart.

Notes

Beginning: The Cravings Begin

1. Robert Robinson, "Come, Thou Fount of Every Blessing," 1758.
2. Psalm 34:8.

Chapter 1—Habit: Habits Are Good Unless They Become Our Habit

1. Romans 7:15 NLT.
2. David Crowder, *Praise Habit: Finding God in Sunsets and Sushi* (Colorado Springs: NavPress, 2004), 25-26.
3. www.urban75.org/useless/bored.html.

Chapter 2—Silence: What We May Hear in the Midst of Silence

1. Matthew 26:38-46 NLT.
2. Mark 2:28 NLT.
3. John 6:53 NLT.
4. John 10:30 NLT.
5. Matthew 9:27-31; 14:13-33; Mark 1:41; John 9:1-7.
6. Matthew 9:18-25; John 11:1-44.
7. Psalm 37:7 NLT; 46:10.
8. 1 Kings 19:12; 1 Samuel 3:4,6,8,10.

Chapter 3—Window: Being Mindful of What Sneaks Through Our Windows

1. Here, I use the term *soul* interchangeably with the term *spirit* to refer to the incorporeal part of humans that will live on for eternity (as opposed to the "seat of our will or emotions"). I do this for the sake of the familiar metaphor, as no one says "the eyes are the windows to the spirit."
2. 1 Corinthians 6:19.
3. Proverbs 4:23 NLT.
4. Job 1:8 NIV.
5. Job 31:1 NIV.
6. Matthew 5:28 NIV.
7. Leviticus 11:44 NLT.
8. Galatians 5:22-23.

Chapter 4—Light: Why Lights Can't Help but Shine Through Darkness

1. Matthew 5:14.
2. C.S. Lewis, *Mere Christianity* (San Francisco: HarperSanFrancisco, 2001), 92.
3. Ephesians 5:11,13.
4. Psalm 27:1; 119:105.
5. Isaiah 9:2; 49:6.
6. John 3:19; 1 John 1:5.
7. Paul adds to the scandal by applying Isaiah's prophecy about being a "light for the Gentiles, that you may bring salvation to the ends of the earth" to the apostles (Acts 13:47).
8. www.reed.edu/apply/student_life/favorite_traditions.html.
9. Matthew 5:15.
10. Matthew 16:24.
11. Matthew 5:39.
12. Matthew 5:42.
13. James 4:8.

Chapter 5—Comfort: Calling All Comfortable Christians

1. Francis Chan, *Crazy Love* (Colorado Springs: Cook, 2008), 96.
2. George Barna, *Revolution* (Wheaton, IL: Tyndale House, 2006), 32.
3. 1 Corinthians 6:19-20.
4. Romans 12:1 NIV.

Chapter 6—Pager: Why We Must Always Answer Our Pagers

1. John 16:7 NIV.

2. Hebrews 11:1.

3. John 4:24; Isaiah 53:2.

4. Hebrews 9:14; Genesis 1:1-2; Luke 1:35 (see Luke 1:32); 1 Corinthians 2:10-11; and Psalm 139:7.

5. When I say "third in line," I am referring to the manner in which our tripartite God has chosen to reveal Himself to mankind. First, God has always existed as one God in three persons, and although the Old Testament shows clear evidence of the Trinity (Genesis 1:1-2; 19:24; Psalm 110:1; 139:1,7; Isaiah 9:6), God was largely understood by the people of the time as a singularity rather than a plurality. He was known as the Creator and the God of Israel, and His presence in the tabernacle and temple brought Him close to mankind. Second, Jesus was revealed in the incarnation as the second person of the Trinity, and Jesus' presence as a man brought God even closer to mankind. Third, the Spirit fills believers and works out God's saving grace within them, and the Spirit's presence has brought God so close to mankind that He dwells within them. So I affirm the historic, orthodox understanding of the Trinity while observing the progression of God's mode of "proximate revelation" throughout human history to demonstrate His tripartite nature.

Chapter 7—Extra: Why Extras Inherit the Kingdom of God

1. Matthew 22:37-39.

2. Luke 6:41.

3. Matthew 7:1; 20:16.

4. Mark 6:34 DARBY.

5. Matthew 6:1,4-6,16-18 NLT.

6. Matthew 5:14-16 NLT.

7. God is unequivocally interested in His own glory because He knows He is the only one worthy of a starring role in this story of human redemption; any other purpose would mean God values something more than Himself, which would be idolatry.

8. Lewis, *Mere Christianity,* 124-25.

9. Romans 12:4-6 NIV.

10. Psalm 96:3; Matthew 28:19-20.

Chapter 8—Different: God Is Different

1. Matthew 25:35,40 NLT.

2. Isaiah 55:9 NLT.

3. 2 Kings 18–20; 2 Chronicles 29–32; Isaiah 36–39.

4. 2 Kings 18:5,7.
5. 2 Kings 20:19.
6. 1 Samuel 13:14.
7. 2 Samuel 12.
8. Genesis 2:8-9,16.
9. Genesis 6:7.
10. Exodus 7–14; Romans 9:17.
11. Acts 4:28.
12. John 3:16.
13. Acts 9:1-19.
14. Ephesians 1:4; 2:8-9.
15. John 14:2-3; 1 Thessalonians 4:16-17; Revelation 21:1-4.
16. A.W. Tozer, *The Knowledge of the Holy* (New York: HarperSanFrancisco, 1992), 1.
17. John Piper, "The State of the Pulpit in America Today" (no longer available online).
18. I have borrowed the phrase "do hard things" from Alex and Brett Harris, authors of *Do Hard Things* (Sisters, OR: Multnomah, 2008), a clarion call for teens to rebel against low expectations in their pursuit of Christ.
19. John 4:10.
20. Romans 8:29.

Chapter 9—Rules: How God Changes All of the Rules

1. Lewis, *Mere Christianity*, 6-7.
2. Romans 10:3.
3. More specifically, I would say the point of rules is to show the need for grace, and thereby our need for Christ, to the praise of His glory. Ultimately, the point of all things is Jesus (see Colossians 1:16).
4. Romans 6:23; 2 Corinthians 5:21; Ephesians 2:8.
5. Romans 7:7.
6. John 14:15.
7. John 14:21,23-24; 15:10.
8. John 15:5.

10. Soldier: How to Find Your Purpose in Combat Boots

1. Mark A. Weitz, *More Damning than Slaughter: Desertion in the Confederate Army* (Lincoln, NE: University of Nebraska Press, 2005), viii.
2. Acts 5:1-11.

3. Matthew 6:9; John 15:15; Romans 8:15,17.

4. John 14:15.

5. Isaiah 6:8.

6. Matthew 6:34.

7. Ephesians 2:10.

8. John Piper makes a small but important amendment to this confession by saying the "chief end of man is to glorify God *by* enjoying Him forever." John Piper, *Desiring God* (Sisters, OR: Multnomah, 2003), 18.

9. Ephesians 1:4-6.

10. Ephesians 2:10.

11. Jonah 2:2,7.

12. Jonah 3:1-3.

13. 2 Timothy 2:3 KJV.

14. 2 Timothy 2:4 WEB.

15. Ephesians 6:10-18.

16. John 1:14.

17. John 7:28; 8:16; 17:18; 1 John 4:10.

18. Luke confirms how "good" of a kid Jesus really was: "And the child grew and became strong, filled with wisdom. And the favor of God was upon him" (Luke 2:40).

19. Luke 2:48.

20. Luke 2:49 NKJV.

21. Luke 2:52.

22. Mark 1:9.

23. Luke 4:1-2.

24. John 4:34.

25. John 6:38.

26. John 5:30 NLT.

27. John 5:19.

28. Mark 6:46; Luke 6:12; 22:39-42.

29. John 14:28.

30. The mission of John Piper's ministry, Desiring God, is particularly appealing to my spiritual affections. It states, "We exist to spread a passion for the supremacy of God in all things for the joy of all peoples through Jesus Christ."

31. Colossians 1:16.

11. Child: Why We Must Act like Children

1. This is why Jesus taught so frequently in parables; He was teaching transcendent, divine truth to limited, mortal men in a way we could understand.

2. Romans 11:33.

3. Romans 1:19-20; 2:14-15; 2 Timothy 3:16.

4. Luke 18:17.

5. Perhaps this is why Compassion International reports that nearly 80 percent of conversions to Christianity occur in children under the age of 12.

6. Having a childlike faith is not simply believing as a child believes; it's also recognizing that adultlike thoughts are infantile when compared to God's. For Paul, to be a child, think like a child, speak like a child, and reason like a child is to be human before an infinitely glorious God (1 Corinthians 13:9-12). John Piper calls this "baby talk" (John Piper, "The Precious Gift of Baby Talk," September 24, 2008, www.desiringgod.org). So we find that childlike faith is a denial of what we perceive to be adultlike, sophisticated spiritual thought and is instead an acknowledgment that our faith is already childish.

7. Proverbs 9:10.

8. Job 11:7 NLT.

9. Isaiah 45:15 NLT.

10. 1 Peter 1:14.

11. C.S. Lewis, *The Chronicles of Narnia: The Last Battle* (New York: HarperCollins, 2001), 744.

12. Ibid., 753.

13. Ibid., 765.

Chapter 12—Hunger: What Hunger Teaches Us About God

1. Brother Yun and Paul Hattaway, *The Heavenly Man* (Mill Hill, London: Monarch Books, 2002), 130-31.

2. Matthew 23:25-26 NIV.

3. Isaiah 29:18; 35:5; 42:7.

4. Matthew 20:29-34.

5. Matthew 9:27-30.

6. Isaiah 42:7; Matthew 12:18-22. See also Luke 4:18.

7. Exodus 7–16.

8. Numbers 11:4-6.

9. Numbers 11:18-20.

10. Deuteronomy 8:2-3.

11. Luke 4:3-4.

12. Matthew 5:6.

13. John 6:27.

14. John 6:32,35.

15. John 6:35,49,51.

16. John 6:53-55.

17. John 6:56.

18. John 15:5,10.

19. John 15:11.

20. Exodus 3:8.

Chapter 13—Suffering: How God Gives Gifts Sometimes

1. Matthew 13:3-4.

2. Matthew 17:20.

3. Matthew 28:20.

4. 2 Corinthians 11:27; 12:9-10.

5. John Piper, *Let the Nations Be Glad* (Grand Rapids: Baker Academic, 2003), 93-94. Originally told by Michael Card, "Wounded in the House of Friends," *Virtue*, March-April 1991, 28-29, 69.

6. Matthew 5:11-12.

7. Matthew 10:22,38; John 15:20.

8. 1 Peter 2:20-21; 4:1.

9. 2 Timothy 3:12; Acts 14:22; Philippians 1:29.

10. Matthew 5:11-12; 1 Peter 4:13; James 1:2.

11. Isaiah 53:3.

12. Colossians 1:24.

13. Billy Orme was kind enough to share his journal with me so I could share it with you. A lot of the thoughts in this chapter came out of discussions I had with Billy, so I'm grateful for his refining input.

14. Job 42:3,6.

15. Romans 8:18.

16. Philippians 3:8.

17. Romans 8:28.

18. See these passages about...
    - God's will in suffering—Philippians 1:29; 1 Peter 2:20-21; 4:19

  • God's purpose in suffering—2 Corinthians 12:9; Colossians 1:24; 2 Timothy 2:10
  • God's sovereignty in suffering—Genesis 50:20; Job 2:6-7,10; Isaiah 45:7

19. James 4:14 NASB.

Chapter 14—Joy: Why God Is to Be Treasured

 1. Luke 2:10; Acts 13:52; 1 Thessalonians 1:6; Hebrews 12:2.

 2. Psalm 51:12; Isaiah 12:3; 35:10; Jeremiah 31:13; Habakkuk 3:18; 1 Peter 1:8-9.

 3. Philippians 2:2; James 1:2; 1 John 1:4.

 4. 1 Kings 1:40; Psalm 66:1; 96:11-12; Isaiah 55:12.

 5. John Piper calls this "Christian hedonism." See *Desiring God*.

 6. Luke 1:44.

 7. Galatians 5:22.

 8. Psalm 21:6; 43:4.

 9. Psalm 16:11.

10. Matthew 13:44.

11. John Piper, *God Is the Gospel* (Wheaton, IL: Crossway Books, 2005), 15.

Other Great
Harvest House Books
You'll Enjoy

Wrestling with Angels
Carolyn Arends

Life is messy. But life is also beautiful. These are the twin themes that author/artist Carolyn Arends (writer of ten Top 10 Christian songs) opens up in her searching exploration of how God meets people in the ordinary moments of life.

I'm Fine with God...It's Christians I Can't Stand
Bruce Bickel and Stan Jantz

Many non-Christians find the behavior of some Christians off-putting rather than inviting. Many Christians do too! This unflinchingly honest and often humorous look at some believers' outlandish behavior empowers Christians to share their faith more freely and helps those who don't yet believe discover the truth about God.

I Can't See God...Because I'm in the Way
Bruce Bickel and Stan Jantz

Bruce and Stan help you understand how you might be getting in your own way of experiencing a heart-igniting faith. This inspiring call to spiritual self-examination will help you replace belief boredom with hunger for God's truth and with the desire to renew your mind and spirit.

Death by Church
Mike Erre

The church is Jesus' hands and feet today. But critics see it as hypocritical, irrelevant, and unloving. Mike Erre, teaching pastor and author of *Jesus of Suburbia* and *Why Guys Need God,* reveals how this has happened and how Christians can more effectively demonstrate Christ's presence in the world.

"

A book is most often a monologue. And that's good at times, because we enjoy listening to the people we read. But sometime monologues can be improved upon. I would love for this book to be a dialogue, to give you the chance to respond, discuss, or challenge what you read. If you're into long dialogues, hopefully we can connect in person one day. If you're into short dialogues, join me at

cravesomethingmore.org

And if you're interested in really short dialogues, there are ways to connect on Facebook and Twitter on this site as well. I hope to hear from you soon, and I hope our conversation will run full with thoughts of Him who satisfies our deepest cravings.

ct